# EDCO
# RELIGIOUS
# EDUCATION
## REVISE WISE

JUNIOR CERTIFICATE HIGHER AND ORDINARY LEVEL

Lori Fields-Whelan and Niamh McDermott

**Edco**
The Educational Company of Ireland

# Contents

Revised

## Section E: The Celebration of Faith

Revised

## Section F: The Moral Challenge

Revised

| Date | | | |
|---|---|---|---|
| Time | | | |
| Section to be revised | | | |

| Date | | | |
|---|---|---|---|
| Time | | | |
| Section to be revised | | | |

| Date | | | |
|---|---|---|---|
| Time | | | |
| Section to be revised | | | |

| Date | | | |
|---|---|---|---|
| Time | | | |
| Section to be revised | | | |

| Date | | | |
|---|---|---|---|
| Time | | | |
| Section to be revised | | | |

| Date | | | |
|---|---|---|---|
| Time | | | |
| Section to be revised | | | |

| Night before exam | |
|---|---|
| Sections to be revised | |

# Introduction

This revision guide will help you to prepare for the Junior Certificate Religious Education examination at both Higher and Ordinary Levels. The main purpose of the book is to reinforce what you have learnt from your detailed standard textbook and to enhance your understanding and skills so that you perform at your optimum level on the day. It contains:

- All material central to the Higher and Ordinary Level syllabus.
- A clear outline of the examination layout.
- Advice on the skills used in the examination.
- Examination questions and answers with guidelines on how they should be answered.

Throughout the book, material which is Higher Level only is denoted by a red line down the side of the page, e.g.:

4 To explore the concepts of leadership, authority and service in communities of faith/churches.

## How to use your Study Plan

A study plan will help you to plan your work coming up to the examination. How to use your Study Plan:

- Plan your work schedule. Do not plan more than you think you will achieve.
- Keep to a daily work timetable.
- Fill in the Study Plan for each day between now and the examination.
- Think positively – remind yourself of the progress you have made and the fact that examiners want students to be successful.
- Study in short bursts interspersed with short breaks.
- As you complete each task that you have set yourself, tick it off. This will make you feel you have made progress.
- If you fall behind in your plan, don't give up! Start again!

## Preparation for the examination day

Get an early night before the examination. You will not perform well if you are tired.

On the day:

1 Follow the instructions in the examination paper.
2 Spend some time deciding which questions you can answer best. It is time well spent.

3    Highlight the key words in the question.

4    Make quick notes on the paper in an effort to structure your answer. This also informs you on whether you are making the right choice.

5    Ensure that you answer the question asked and that your answer stays relevant.

6    Time yourself throughout the examination.

7    Answer first the questions you know most about. Leave until last the one you are least happy with.

8    Leave enough time at the end to read through your answers and make minor corrections if needed.

9    Remember, presentation, including handwriting, is important. Take care with both.

**Your revision notes**

# Examination Section

## The Examination Paper

Religious Education may be taken at either Higher or Ordinary Level. At each level there is one written examination paper. There are 400 marks available for the written paper. You are allowed 2 hours to complete the paper. The time and marks are allocated as follows:

### Higher Level

| Section | Time Allowed | Marks Available |
|---------|-------------|-----------------|
| 1 | 15 minutes | 50 marks |
| 2 | 15 minutes | 30 marks |
| 3 | 15 minutes | 50 marks |
| 4 | 55 minutes | 200 marks |
| 5 | 20 minutes | 70 marks |

### Ordinary Level

| Section | Time Allowed | Marks Available |
|---------|-------------|-----------------|
| 1 | 20 minutes | 80 marks |
| 2 | 20 minutes | 60 marks |
| 3 | 20 minutes | 60 marks |
| 4 | 60 minutes | 200 marks |

## General Preparation

- Be familiar with the different styles of questions asked in each section of the examination.
- Practice each of the sections beforehand using past examination papers.

- Follow the instructions given at the beginning of each section on the examination paper with regard to the time you should spend on each section and the amount of questions you are required to answer.
- Ensure that you have revised the key concepts for each section of the syllabus.

# Examination Paper – Section by Section

## Section 1

- In this section there are **20** questions. You must answer **10** of these.
- To give yourself the best possible chance of gaining full marks in this section, answer as many questions as you can.
- Be sure to answer all the multiple choice or tick the box questions. Even if you are not sure of the answer, guess. You might be right!
- However, be clear in your answering. For example, if you are asked to identify or tick one right answer be sure to only mark one. Ticking all the options will not earn you any marks.
- If a definition is required be sure that you give a full and relevant one.

## Section 2

- There are **4** questions in this section. You must answer **3** of these. Only answer all 4 if you have enough time.
- You will be provided with pictures in this question. Look at them carefully. They are there to help you with your answer.
- Sometimes the pictures show an example of a particular thing. The question may ask you to give **another** example. Be careful that you do not repeat what is already shown in the picture.

## Section 3

- In this section of the examination you will be given a piece of text to read and then you must answer questions about the text.
- Make sure you read the piece of text more than once. Read the questions and then re-read the piece of text, underlining any key sentences you think might be relevant to your answers.
- You must refer directly to the piece of text in each of your answers.
- Pay particular attention to the last question. In previous years the question has required candidates to explain a concept and then show how it is represented in the piece of text. If you are asked to do this, make sure you remember to answer both parts of the question.

## Section 4

- There are **6** questions in this section. At **Ordinary Level** you must answer **5** questions and at **Higher Level** you must answer **4** questions.
- Read all the questions before you select which ones you will answer.

- Each question relates to a different part of the syllabus. This means the questions will be based on the following areas: Communities, Christianity, Major World Religions, Faith, Worship and Morality.
- Pick your questions from the sections or areas you know best.
- Usually there are different parts to each of these questions. Make sure you answer each part.

## Section 5

- **This section only appears on the Higher Level paper.**
- There are **6** questions in this section. You must answer **1** of these.
- As with **Section 4** there will be a question about each of the following: Communities, Christianity, Major World Religions, Faith, Worship and Morality.
- Sometimes you are given a number of tasks to do in a single question. Read the question you choose carefully and identify what it is asking you to do. If you do not address all parts of the question in your answer you will not be awarded full marks.
- As this is an essay style question it may be helpful to make an essay plan.

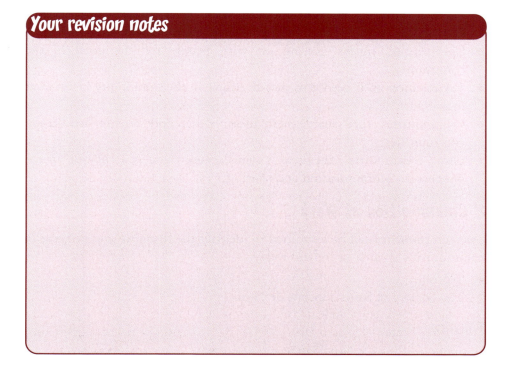

**Points to note**

REVISE WISE
POINTS TO NOTE

Remember quality not quantity in this question!

**Your revision notes**

### ●●● Learning Objectives

**In this chapter you will learn about:**

1. The nature and pattern of human communities
2. Identifying the characteristics of communities of faith/churches
3. These characteristics as they occur in communities of faith/churches in local, national and international examples
4. The concepts of leadership, authority and service in communities of faith/churches

## 1 Community

- A community is a group of people who have something in common.
- We all belong to different types of community: national, international or local, e.g. St Vincent de Paul, Amnesty International, Residents Association, Meals on wheels.
- Every person who belongs to a community has an important **role** or part to play in the community.
- For a community to work properly there needs to be **co-operation**, **communication** and **sharing** between all its members.
- Co-operation means getting on with people for the good of the community.
- Communication is needed so that all people in the community know what is going on.
- Communities that share their ideas, skills and talents are strong communities.
- Often communities can break down because there is a collapse in co-operation, communication and sharing.

## 2 Communities at Work

Two communities can be examined to identify the meaning and purpose of communities of faith in Ireland today:

- Trócaire.
- The Society of Saint Vincent de Paul.

## Trócaire

In the Irish language the word Trócaire means compassion. Trócaire was set up in 1973 by the Irish Catholic Bishops to show the concern of the Irish church for the world's poorest people. Trócaire supports long-term development projects overseas and provides relief when necessary during emergencies. It is the official overseas development agency of the Catholic Church in Ireland and raises public awareness of worldwide poverty. Trócaire tries to live out the message of the Gospels each day in the work that it does. Jesus himself heard the poor cry, so today Trócaire hopes for a better world where resources are shared and people are free to make their own destiny. Trócaire helps communities in their efforts to improve their lives while at the same time respects the human dignity of all. The most high profile public awareness campaign Trócaire has run was for the Tsunami in South East Asia in December 2004. Trócaire sent financial aid and technical support immediately to the most needed areas.

Trócaire listens to the people it works with as they are the focus of it's work. The needs and opinions of these people are put first so that the right solutions are found – Trócaire helps people to help themselves. Trócaire understands that there are no quick-fix solutions to the world's problems and there is still so much to do to make the world a fairer and better place to live.

## The Society of Saint Vincent de Paul

The Society of Saint Vincent de Paul is a Christian organisation working with the poor and disadvantaged people in society. The organisation brings the love of Christ to those who need it in society. Many join the organisation as they want to spread the message of Jesus Christ on earth by showing love and care to the disadvantaged. The organisation believes that all people should be loved and as a result, the organisation offers friendship and support to people in need. Each volunteer takes on a role, whether that is visiting people in their home, hospital or prison or helping a child at school. The organisation's work involves person to person contact and the organisation is committed to respecting the dignity of all people. Many people depend on the volunteer's generous giving of time and kindness. The work of the organisation is completely confidential.

## Needs and wants

There is much poverty and deprivation in the world, but people still want things that they do not really need. Access to shelter and a regular meal are the basic necessities, but many of us want more than this.

## 3 Communities of Faith and Leadership

- Communities of faith are organisations where people come together and show a commitment to their religious beliefs.
- The Loreto Order is an example of a community of faith. Members of the Loreto Order work at local, national and international level. Education is

a central part of the work of the Loreto Order, but the Order is also involved in parish work. It tries to help people in their faith development through retreat work and spiritual development. The Loreto sisters are also involved in missionary work as their members have travelled all over the world to pray, work and teach. God is the driving force of this community of faith.

## Points to note

**Mission** means putting religious beliefs into practice.

- The Church of Ireland is also an important community of faith. It is a Protestant Church but has a lot in common with the Catholic Church. The Church of Ireland is made up of individuals who care about the world. Its members serve God and in doing so demonstrate God's love through their members' interaction with and treatment of people of all faiths.

## Points to note

**Denomination** means belonging to a particular branch of a religion.

## Leadership

Every community or group needs certain things if it is to work properly and reach its full potential. We need to co-operate and communicate with each other and one way of ensuring this is to have strong **leadership**. A leader is someone who guides their community because they are given the position of **authority**. Different styles of leadership are often used by people in that position:

- **Authoritarian**: A leader tells the members of a community what to do without asking for their opinion. When this style of leadership is used correctly it can be effective as it gets things done and avoids errors. However, it does not work for all communities.
- **Democratic**: A leader encourages the members of the community to be involved in the running and the decision-making of the community. For this type of leadership to be effective there needs to be trust between all members.
- **Free reign**: A leader hands over control to the members. This type of leadership is effective as it lets members feel valued and trusted, but if there are no structures in place it can be ineffective.

## Leadership in the Church of Ireland

- Every community of faith is organised and run in a certain way.
- The leadership style of the Church of Ireland is democratic.

- The joint leaders are the Archbishop of Armagh and the Archbishop of Dublin. They consult with the other bishops and represent the Church for many international bodies.
- The Most Rev. John Neill is the current Archbishop of Dublin and Primate of Ireland. The current Archbishop of Armagh and Primate of All Ireland is the Most Rev. Alan Harper.
- The leadership of this Church involves both laity and clergy and everyone's views are represented.

## Leadership in the Roman Catholic Church

The Roman Catholic Church is the largest Christian Church in the world. The mission of the Catholic Church covers the whole world and does not exclude any country or race. In the Catholic Church everyone has a role to play. People can serve God in different ways:

- The Pope is head of the Catholic Church worldwide and serves God this way. The Pope lives in the Vatican in Rome which is the headquarters of the Catholic Church. Catholics believe that the Pope is the successor to St Peter on earth. When the Pope dies his successor is chosen from one of the Cardinals.
- Cardinals are given their position by the Pope. They are the chief advisers to the Pope on all religious matters.
- Archbishops are the religious leaders of a particular country. Bishops have the important role of the religious leader of a diocese. There are 26 dioceses in Ireland. The bishop confirms people at confirmation time.
- Priests are the religious leaders of a parish. They celebrate the sacraments of baptism, Eucharist, sacrament of the sick, marriage and reconciliation with their congregation.
- The laity or lay people are those who have not been ordained to religious life or priesthood but still have a leadership role in the Catholic Church. The lay person can read at mass, give out communion or help with the parish centre.

# 4 Relationships between Communities of Faith

For many years the Christian Churches (Catholics, Protestants and Orthodox Christians) worked against each other. Today this is very different as they communicate with each other and join in ceremonies together. This is called Ecumenism.

## Ecumenism

Ecumenism is the attempt that Christians make to understand and respect each other and to grow more as one. Ecumenism promotes mutual respect and understanding between the Christian Churches through dialogue. It also encourages all Christians to co-operate with each other and so spread the love that Christ has for each of us. An example of ecumenism is the Taizé community in France. The Corrymeela Community in County Antrim is another example of ecumenism in action.

### Taizé

- Young people from all walks of life and all parts of the world go to Taizé to deepen their faith.
- The Brothers of Taizé belong to all the Christian Churches.
- Taizé gives people a chance to think about their lives.
- Prayer is an important aspect of Taizé as people come together during the day to pray and sing.
- Taizé gives people hope.

### Sectarianism

Sectarianism is the hatred of someone because of their religion. The causes of sectarianism are deep and complex. Communities can become deeply divided as a result of sectarianism as it can lead to mistrust amongst community members. When it is at its worst it can be difficult to heal.

## Interfaith dialogue

**Interfaith dialogue** is similar to ecumenism but there is an important difference between the two.

- Interfaith dialogue is communication and understanding between people from different major world religions, not just the Christian Churches.
- The **World Council of Churches** is a group that aims to bring about peace and understanding between different faiths. The aim is to build trust and face common challenges together through dialogue. During the past few years, it has organised a number of Hindu-Christian, Christian-Muslim, Buddhist-Christian and Jewish-Christian dialogues.
- **World Day of Peace:** This began in Assisi in Italy in 1986. It was organised by Pope John Paul II as part of the World Day of Peace. He invited all the leaders of different religions to come together to pray for peace in the world. On this day, every religion listens to the prayers of the others.

### Points to note

**Sectarianism** means the hatred of someone because of their religious beliefs.

- The key to solving **sectarianism** is through tolerance. Religious conflict can cause division within a community.
- **Tolerance** is about respect for and communication with one another. It is important to foster and encourage tolerance from a young age.
- Sectarianism can also be prevented by encouraging people to get involved in ecumenism and interfaith dialogue.

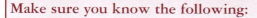

## Key Points

**Make sure you know the following:**

### 1 Community

- Co-operation and lack of co-operation
- Sharing
- Communication
- Roles
- Community breakdown

### 2 Communities at work

- Commitment
- Service
- Vision
- Leadership

### 3 Communities of faith and leadership

- Denomination
- Religious commitment
- Mission
- Leadership
- Authority

### 4 Relationships between communities of faith

- Ecumenism
- Interfaith dialogue
- Sectarianism
- Tolerance
- Religious conflict

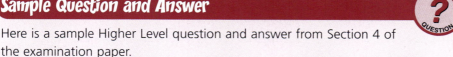

## Sample Question and Answer

Here is a sample Higher Level question and answer from Section 4 of the examination paper.

## 2005, HL, Section 4, Q1

### Communities of Faith

A. "Archbishop Eames calls for 'determined effort' to end sectarianism"
   - *Irish Times*, December 2004

a. What is sectarianism? (5 marks)

*Sectarianism is the hatred of someone because of their religion.*

b. Outline **one** example of sectarianism. (10 marks)

*When we hear the word sectarianism we are immediately reminded of the troubles in the North between Catholics and Protestants. Since the 1960s there has been a lot of trouble between the two communities living in the six counties. People living in Northern Ireland were afraid, angry and suspicious of each other. Today Catholics and Protestants can live side by side due to the Good Friday Agreement. This was 10 years old on 10 April 2008. Those living in the North today respect the religious differences of others and there is no longer intolerance or violence towards those who come from another Christian religion.*

c. Identify **two** effects sectarianism can have on a community of faith. (10 marks)

## Sample Question and Answer *(Continued)*

*i.* One effect that sectarianism can have on a community of faith is a lack of trust of your neighbour. This is because of all the trouble in the community.

*ii.* Another effect that sectarianism can have on the community is hatred towards each other. Because of this communities become divided and this leads to tension.

B. a. What is ecumenism? (5 marks)

Ecumenism is the attempt that Christians make to understand and respect each other and to grow more as one.

b. Briefly outline **one** example of ecumenism. (10 marks)

One example of ecumenism is Taizé. This is a community in France where all young people of different Christian denominations come together to pray and learn about the Christian faith. In Taizé everyone helps with the daily chores. The most important aim of the community is to work for Christian unity.

c. Give **two** reasons why people work for ecumenism. (10 marks)

One reason why people work for ecumenism is to promote respect between different Christian communities.

Another reason is to encourage co-operation between the different Christian churches.

## Questions

### Section 1 Questions

1  A community to which I belong is_____. (5 marks)
2  In religious traditions sectarianism means_____. (5 marks)
3  Tolerance between communities of faith can be seen when people are willing to respect different religious beliefs and opinions. Is this true or false? (5 marks)

   True ☐                              False ☐

4  Name a Christian denomination that exists in Ireland:_____. (5 marks)

### Section 2 Questions
### 2005, HL, Section 2, Q1

This is a photograph of Archbishop Diarmuid Martin introducing Bono from the pop group U2, to Pope John Paul II.

1  Pick **one** thing from the photograph which shows that Archbishop Diarmuid Martin is a religious leader in a community of faith. (2 marks)

## Questions *(Continued)*

2 "Archbishop" and "Pope" are titles given to religious leaders. State **one** other title given to the leader of a community of faith you have studied.

(2 marks)

3 Briefly outline the role of a religious leader in a community of faith you have studied. (6 marks)

## Section 3 Question
### 2004, OL, Section 3

The following is an interview given by a young person after a visit to Taizé.

My Trip To Taizé

Interviewer: You've just finished a visit to Taizé. Did you enjoy it?

Ger: Yes, as you will see from my photos, I met lots of people from all over the world.

Interviewer: Why do so many young people go to Taizé?

Ger: People go there for different reasons. Some are searching for meaning; others are looking for a deeper relationship with God. Some come for a chance to meet other Christians of their own age, or for an experience of living with a community rooted in the Gospel. The religious brothers who live in Taizé share their life and faith with all who visit. Everyone is made feel welcome in Taizé.

Interviewer: What type of person goes to Taizé?

Ger: Some of the people I met are active in churches at home, others find it difficult to find a church where they feel welcomed and listened to.

Interviewer: What did you do during the day?

Ger: Most days I had some practical tasks to do, like cooking and cleaning. But, no matter what I was doing, I would go to the Church of Reconciliation three times a

## Questions (Continued)

day and join the community in worship. I also attended Bible meetings that the brothers held each day.

Interviewer: What did you like best about being in Taizé?

Ger: I enjoyed the time for reflection and I liked hearing about other people's hopes and beliefs. I liked the meditation too, which had a lot of singing and silence. The music was great. The brothers make up simple tunes using a few words that you can learn easily.

At prayer you sing these tunes over and over again. Anyone can join in, it doesn't matter what language you speak.

Interviewer: How did your week in Taizé help you?

Ger: Listening to people my own age talking about their search for meaning and faith has changed my whole way of thinking about life.

Interviewer: Would you go there again?

Ger: Yes. It was great. It gave me a chance to relax and think about life. I made good friends. We still keep in touch and we'll meet again soon.

1 From your reading of this interview give **two** reasons why people go to Taizé. (28 marks)

2 During the visit to Taizé, Ger took part in different religious activities. Tick **one** of the following activities and explain why people would choose to express their faith in this way.

Praying with the community ☐       Going to Bible meetings ☐
Discussing religious topics ☐                    (12 marks)

3 Tick **one** of the following and explain what it means.

Religious commitment ☐       Inspiring vision ☐
Vocation ☐                             (10 marks)

4 Describe how what you have ticked above is shown in what Ger said about Taizé. (10 marks)

## Section 4 Questions

1 Name a church or religious organisation or a religious order found in present-day Ireland, and outline **two** ways in which its beliefs influence the way of life of its members.

2 Outline one challenge that a church/religious organisation/religious order faces in Ireland today.

3 Briefly outline how the beliefs of the church/religious organisation/the religious order you have named above could help its members to deal with the challenge.

## Section 5 Questions

1 Outline one example of interfaith dialogue that you have studied.

2 Discuss the reasons why people take part in interfaith dialogue.

## ●●●Learning Objectives

**In this chapter you will learn about:**

1 The context in which Jesus was born
2 Identification of the Gospels as the main source of knowledge about Jesus
3 The meaning of the life, death and resurrection of Jesus for his followers, then and now
4 Understanding the meanings attached to the new titles for Jesus

# 1 The Context of Jesus' Birth

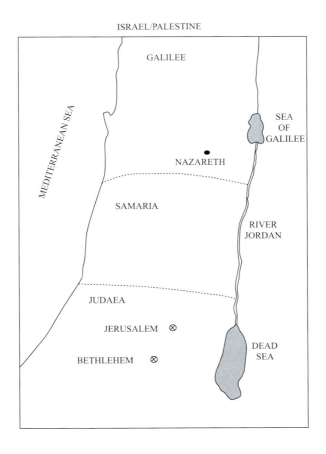

The map on page 15 shows some of the most important places associated with the life of Jesus.

1 **Galilee, Samaria and Judaea:** The three provinces of Palestine.
2 **Bethlehem:** The birthplace of Jesus.
3 **Nazareth:** The town where Jesus grew up.
4 **River Jordan:** The river where Jesus was baptised.
5 **Sea of Galilee:** The place where Jesus met his first disciples.
6 **Jerusalem:** The town where Jesus was arrested and put to death and where his resurrection took place.

## Points to note

REVISE WISE
POINTS TO NOTE

The region where Jesus lived, preached and died became known as the **Holy Land.**

## The Roman Empire

- Palestine was under the control of the **Roman Empire** at the time of Jesus.
- The Jewish people wanted an independent land they could call their own and rule over themselves.
- The Jewish people were waiting on a Messiah, who would free them from Roman rule and establish a new Jewish Kingdom.
- They saw the Messiah as the anointed one sent by God, who would lead them to freedom. They expected he would be a strong warrior-like person. Until he came they were to follow the rules and laws given to them by the prophet Moses (see page 34).

## Ancient Judaism

Ancient Judaism refers to the history of the Jewish people, including their politics, culture and religion.

### Political and religious structures

1 **The Sadducees:** A powerful, wealthy group. They held the position of high priest in Jerusalem and collected the temple taxes. They were happy to be ruled by the Romans because they felt the Romans brought stability and wealth to Palestine.
2 **The Zealots:** They hated the Romans and were willing to use violence to rid Palestine of foreign rulers and defend the Jewish faith.
3 **The Pharisees:** The religious leaders of the synagogue. They followed the religious law above everything else. They believed that God would send the Messiah to free them from foreign rule.

4   **The Essenes:** They led a simple, monk-like, life in remote places and followed the teachings of the Torah closely.

5   **The Sanhedrin:** An assembly of Jews who upheld the religious laws. They could not interfere in civil matters. The Romans accepted them because they did not want to get involved in religious law and because the Sanhedrin helped to keep the peace in Palestine.

6   **Tax Collectors:** Collected money from the people to support the Roman army in Palestine. They were often wealthy but were disliked by the ordinary Jews because they worked with the Romans.

7   **The Temple:** The most sacred place for Jews in Jerusalem. They visited it especially during religious festivals to pray and offer sacrifices to their God. Parts of it became used as trading areas. Only temple coins could be used here. The High Priests and scribes taught here.

8   **The Synagogue:** Sacred buildings found in most towns. Jews worshipped here at the weekly Sabbath. The rabbi taught the Jewish people the scriptures that were kept here on scrolls in a special place called The Ark.

## 2 Evidence about Jesus

Make sure you know the following:

- **The Bible:** A collection of books split into two parts: The Old Testament and The New Testament.
- **The Old Testament:** Also known as the Hebrew Scriptures. It traces the history of the Jewish people. It contains the stories of the **prophets** who spoke to the people on behalf of God.
- **The New Testament:** Tells the story of Jesus' life, death and resurrection and the beginnings of Christianity. There are four **Gospels**.
- **Gospel:** The word means Good News. They are stories of the teachings of Jesus as well as the events of his death and resurrection.
- **The Evangelists:** Another name for the **four** Gospel writers. They were Matthew, Mark, Luke and John.
- **Evidence from oral to written traditions:** Information about Jesus went from the spoken to the written word.

## Sources of evidence

### The Bible

The Gospels came about in three stages:

1   The actual events during Jesus' life: He preached about the kingdom of God through parables, miracles and table fellowship. The disciples travelled with him and witnessed all he did.

2   The disciples preaching about Jesus: The Holy Spirit gave the Apostles the courage to travel far and wide telling people the Good News that Jesus had taught them. It was passed from one person to the next by word of mouth. This is called the **oral** stage.

3   The writing down of the Gospels: As the Good News travelled further it became impossible for the Apostles to preach and teach in person. Also they were growing older and dying. So they had to write the Good News down before it was too late. This meant it would never be forgotten.

### Historical documents about Jesus

### Josephus

A Jewish scholar and historian who wrote a book 60 years after the death of Jesus about the history of the Jews. In it he says Jesus was a teacher who was crucified and rose from the dead three days later.

### Tacitus

A Roman historian who mentions Jesus in his writings 80 years after his death. Unlike the Gospel writers both these men were concerned with facts. Their work shows that Jesus was a real person who did exist.

### The four Gospel writers

### Matthew

Wrote his Gospel for the Jewish Christians and his symbol was the Angel. Saw Jesus as the new Moses, the promised one sent by God.

### Mark

Wrote his Gospel for the Christians living in Rome and his symbol was the Lion. Focuses on Jesus as a teacher and miracle worker.

### Luke

Wrote his Gospel for the Gentiles (non Jews) and his symbol was the bull. Describes Jesus as a man of prayer and someone who loved the poor and oppressed.

### John

Wrote his Gospel for the Christians in the Mediterranean world and his symbol was the eagle. He saw Jesus as a real human being and yet the real Son of God. John wrote stories that are not found in the other three Gospels.

## Points to note

The word **synoptic** means describing events from a similar point of view.

### The Synoptic Gospels

The Gospels of Matthew, Mark and Luke are all similar and therefore are called the **Synoptic Gospels**. Matthew and Luke used Mark's Gospel when writing theirs. They also used a document called Quelle or the Q document. This was a collection of Jesus' sayings written years before.

# 3 The Person and Preaching of Jesus

Make sure you know the following:

- **The kingdom of God:** A way of living based on Jesus' message of truth, justice, peace and love. Jesus used parables, miracles and table fellowship to teach people how to live as God wants them to.

## Points to note

**Table fellowship** – Jesus chose to share his meals with all to show that God's kingdom was for everyone.

- **Parable:** A short story based on earth with a message about heaven. Jesus used parables as the kingdom of God was a difficult thing for people to understand. Parables got the people's attention and challenged their faith. An example of a parable would be **the Good Samaritan.**

**The parable of the Good Samaritan: Luke 10: 25-37.** A man was robbed and left half dead on the side of the road. People passed him by without helping. A Samaritan stopped and tended to the man's wounds. Samaritans were disliked at the time by the other Jews as they had different customs and mixed with non Jews. This parable shows that anyone can be a member of the kingdom of God. Being a good neighbour has nothing to do with your race or religion.

- **Miracle:** An amazing event performed by Jesus that showed the power of God. The three types of miracles are the miracles of **healing**, the miracles of **nature** and the miracles of **exorcism**.

**The miracle of the calming of the storm: Mark 4: 35-41.** The Apostles and Jesus left the crowds and went in their boats. A great gale began to blow and toss the boat as Jesus slept. The Apostles woke him in a panic. He told the sea and winds to be calm and the storm obeyed. The Apostles were amazed.

- **Table fellowship:** At the time of Jesus people only shared meals with people who were of the same class as them in society. Jesus ate with people who were seen as outcasts in society, such as Zacchaeus the tax collector, to show people that the kingdom of God was for everyone no matter what class they belonged to.
- **Discipleship:** Being a disciple is all about change and wanting to become a better and more holy person. It means following the call of Jesus in thought, mind and deed.

- **Vocation:** Means being called to serve God. All Christians are called to serve God. They can do this in many ways such as helping those less fortunate.
- **Mission:** Something we stand up for because we really believe in it. The mission of a disciple is to stand up for the kingdom of God.

## 4 The Death and Resurrection of Jesus

**Make sure you know the following:**

- **Conflict with authority:** Jesus clashed with certain groups of people who felt threatened by him and his message. One such group was the Pharisees.
- **Jesus and the Pharisees:** The Pharisees disliked Jesus because they felt he ignored the Law, which they followed above all else. They thought they were the ones who knew the most about God and how to follow him. They felt Jesus threatened the religious power they held.
- **Holy Week:** Events remembered every year at Easter time when Christians all over the world take part in ceremonies to commemorate them.

### The events of Holy Week

**Sunday:** Known as Palm Sunday. Jesus entered Jerusalem on a donkey as the people gathered to celebrate the festival of **Passover:** The crowds waved palm branches and cried, 'Hosanna' like they were welcoming a new king. This unsettled the Sanhedrin.

**Monday:** Jesus went to the Temple and overturned the tables of the money changers. He drove out the people who had turned this holy place into a place of trade and money-making. The Sadducees were angered as they did not want things to change because they were making money out of the Temple.

**Tuesday:** Jesus taught in the Temple. The Pharisees and Sadducees asked him questions to try and catch him out. They questioned him about paying taxes. If he said it was wrong to pay taxes he would have been in trouble with the Romans. But if he said it was right it would be like saying the Emperor was more important than God. But he was not afraid and gave a clever answer saying, 'Pay the Emperor what belongs to the Emperor and pay to God what belongs to God'. This way he did not offend anyone. This angered the leaders even more.

**Wednesday:** Judas, one of the 12 Apostles, met with the High Priests in secret and offered to help them arrest Jesus. In exchange for 30 pieces of silver he would identify Jesus for them at night to avoid a big public scene.

**Thursday:** The Last Supper took place. Jesus had gathered with the Apostles to celebrate the Passover meal. Jesus washed the feet of his disciples. He was showing them that being a good disciple meant serving others. He then told them that one of them would betray him. The Apostles were shocked and would not believe him. He then took bread, gave thanks, broke it, blessed it and gave it to his disciples saying, 'This is my body, given up for you. Do this in memory of me.' Then he did the same with the cup, saying it was his blood.

The Last Supper was a meal in the Passover tradition. At the Passover, a lamb was sacrificed to symbolise the Israelite's freedom. At the Last Supper Jesus is the new lamb, sacrificed for the sins of the world. Also the Passover was a memorial meal and Jesus said, 'Do this in memory of me.' Both meals celebrate something that happened in the past but celebrate what they mean in the present too. After the meal Jesus and his Apostles went to the Garden of Gethsemane to pray. Jesus prayed to God for strength as he knew what was going to happen. Judas arrived, went up to Jesus and kissed him on the cheek. This was the sign for the Jewish leaders to make their arrest. He was taken to the High Priest for his trial to begin.

**Friday:** Jesus was brought before Pontius Pilate. But Pilate did not want to get involved so he sent him to Herod, the ruler of Galilee, the place where Jesus was from. Herod just mocked Jesus and sent him back to Pilate. Pilate could find no reason to condemn Jesus as he had not broken any laws. However, he did not want to annoy the Jewish leaders and people. Pilate offered the people a choice; he would free Jesus or Barabbas, a common criminal. The people chose Barabbas and when asked about Jesus they shouted, 'Crucify him!'

Jesus was whipped and beaten and had a crown of thorns put on his head. He was then made to carry a heavy cross through the streets. He stumbled and a man from the crowd called Simon was made to help him. Some of his followers along the way cried and mourned. At Calvary, Jesus was nailed to the cross to die. His last words were, 'Father, into your hands I place my spirit.' Jesus' body was taken from the cross by some of his followers. It was wrapped in a shroud and placed in a tomb. It was agreed that some of the women who followed Jesus would return on the Sunday, after the Sabbath, and prepare the body for proper burial.

**Saturday:** Jesus' followers were frightened and confused. They could not believe their leader was gone. They were angry that he had left them and afraid that they might be punished because they had followed him. They also felt great sadness as their friend whom they loved had been taken from them. They wondered how they would carry on.

**Sunday:** Mary Magdalene and some of the other women returned to the tomb. They saw that the big rock in front of it had been moved and the tomb was empty. The women were frightened and confused and left to tell the others.

- **The Resurrection:** Jesus was restored to life three days after he had died.
- **The Risen Jesus:** Jesus approached his followers. One of the first people he appeared to was Mary Magdalene. His followers did not recognise him at first as he had changed in some way. He reassured them saying, 'Peace be with you.' Their fear was replaced by joy as they realised their master had not left them. He gave them instructions to go and do his work.

- **Transformation:** The change that occurred in Jesus after the resurrection making him present among his followers in a new way.
- **Presence:** Jesus' presence (existence) after the resurrection was an everlasting one.

## 5 Faith in Christ

**Make sure you know the following:**

- **The Ascension:** For forty days after the resurrection Jesus continued to appear to his followers and told them to wait in Jerusalem for a gift from his father. He was then taken up to Heaven (ascended), body and soul.
- **Pentecost:** All the believers were gathered together in a room. A noise like a loud wind blowing came and tongues of fire appeared above each person. They were all filled with the Holy Spirit. This gave them the courage to go out and preach the word of God and baptise others in the name of Jesus.
- **Missionary work:** Continuing Jesus' work on earth.
- **The first Christian communities:** Peter was the first Apostle to preach to large crowds. Many people were baptised and the first Christian communities were formed. They were a close group. They spent their time together sharing ideas about God and praying. They tried to live as Jesus had. They shared all their possessions and all treated each other fairly. Most importantly they remembered Jesus' words and actions at the Last Supper. This meal of thanksgiving became known as the **Eucharist**.
- **Martyrdom:** A martyr is someone who is willing to suffer and even die for their religious beliefs. One such person was a disciple called Stephen. The disciples who preached were soon in trouble with the authorities who had been in conflict with Jesus. They did not want the disciples carrying on his work. Stephen was brought before the elders but the Holy Spirit gave him the strength to carry on. He was stoned to death – Stephen had been willing to die for his faith.
- **St Paul:** A man named Saul was among those persecuting the first Christians. One day he was on his way to a city called Damascus to look for followers of Jesus. Suddenly a light from the sky blinded him and he heard the voice of Jesus. For three days he remained blind. A man named Ananias came and told him he must do God's work. Saul got his sight back, was baptised and became known as Paul. Paul travelled to lots of different Christian communities, helping them to become united and strong.

## Different names used to refer to Jesus

Jesus is known by many different names and titles. This helps people to understand the different sides to his personality.

- **Son of Man:** This title appears in the Gospel of Mark. Jesus himself used it. It means that Jesus came in human form to serve man. An Old Testament prophet Daniel had used this title when referring to the Messiah.
- **Son of God:** The early Church used this title to show that they believed Jesus had a special relationship with God. It shows that Jesus was divine as well as human.

- **New Creation:** Jesus, who was totally different to any other human, was an amazing and unique being that God had given to his people. St Paul used this title when talking about Jesus.
- **Christ/Messiah:** The anointed one. It shows that the people believed that Jesus was the one they had been waiting for. Anointed people had a special authority from God. This title meant that Jesus was the Messiah who had come to save the people.

## Key Points

**Make sure you know the following:**

**1 The context of Jesus' birth**
- The Holy Land
- The Roman Empire
- Ancient Judaism

**2 Evidence about Jesus**
- Evidence from the oral and written traditions
- Gospel
- Evangelist
- Synoptic

**3 The person and preaching of Jesus**
- Parable
- Miracle
- Table fellowship
- Discipleship
- Vocation
- Mission

**4 The death and resurrection of Jesus**
- Conflict with authority
- Martyrdom
- Passover
- Eucharist
- Resurrection
- Transformation
- Presence

**5 Faith in Christ**
- Pentecost
- Missionary
- Son of Man
- Son of God
- New Creation
- Christ/Messiah

## Sample Question and Answer

Here is a sample Higher Level question and answer from Section 4 of the examination paper.

### 2005, HL, Section 4, Q2

**Foundations of Religion – Christianity**

A. a. Below you will find a list of some of the events leading up to the death of Jesus. Number these events in the order in which they occurred. Number **1** should be the first event and number **5** should be the last event. (10 marks)

## Sample Question and Answer (Continued)

| Number | Event |
|--------|-------|
| 5 | The Crucifixion |
| 4 | Jesus is brought to Pontius Pilate |
| 3 | Jesus is brought before the Sanhedrin |
| 1 | The Last Supper |
| 2 | Temple guards arrest Jesus |

b. What was the role of the Sanhedrin in Palestine at the time of Jesus? (6 marks)

*The Sanhedrin was the Jewish court of law in Palestine. It only dealt with religious laws and did not have the authority to interfere in civil matters. It did not have the power to put people to death. The Romans were happy for the Sanhedrin to help keep the peace.*

c. What position did Pontius Pilate hold in the political life of Palestine at the time of Jesus? (6 marks)

*Pontius Pilate was the Governor of Judaea and Samaria. He was appointed by the Romans to rule their lands for them. Jesus was brought before him for a trial.*

B. Imagine you were **one** of the disciples who witnessed Jesus' death and were present when Jesus appeared after his resurrection.

a. Describe the impact that the death of Jesus had on your life. (12 marks)

*I could not believe it when Jesus was crucified. He had been my teacher and friend. I was heartbroken at the thought of not seeing him again. To see him scorned and beaten was very hard. To be crucified is a horrible way to die. I was also a bit angry. Jesus was supposed to be our leader and now he is gone. Who will lead us now? I am a bit scared that the same thing might happen to me.*

b. Describe **one** of the appearances of the risen Jesus you witnessed and the effect it had on you. (16 marks)

*I was walking along the road with some friends. A man came along and began talking to us. We did not recognise him at first. Then he began to say and do things that reminded us of our master. We were confused and scared. But he said, 'Peace be with you' and suddenly we knew our master was back. We were not frightened anymore. We were excited that Jesus was again among us. He told us to go and preach the good news. I felt like I could do anything and I rushed off to tell others about what had happened.*

## Questions

### Section 1 Questions

### 2004, HL, Section 1, Q7

An historical source of evidence for the life of Jesus is – (Tick the correct box)

Jacob ☐      Job ☐      Josephus ☐      Joshua ☐      (5 marks)

## Questions *(Continued)*

### 2005, HL, Section 1, Q8

The people who held political power in Palestine at the time of Jesus were –
(Tick the correct box)

Assyrians ☐     Egyptians ☐     Greeks ☐          Romans ☐          (5 marks)

### 2005, HL, Section 1, Q15

One example of martyrdom from the founding story of Christianity is_____

_____.

(5 marks)

### 2006, HL, Section 1, Q16

At the time of Jesus, Jerusalem was in the province of _____.

(5 marks)

### 2007, HL, Section 1, Q18

The Gospel of Mark is a synoptic gospel. (Tick the correct box)     (5 marks)

True  ☐          False  ☐

## Section 2 Questions

### 2004, OL, Section 2, Q1

This is a photograph of a Holy Week
procession in Spain.

A. State **one** thing from the photograph
   which suggests that Holy Week is a time
   of significance.          (6 marks)

B. Holy Week is a time of significance for
   which one of the following world religions
   (Tick the correct box)          (6 marks)
   Buddhism  ☐          Christianity  ☐
   Hinduism  ☐          Islam          ☐          Judaism  ☐

C. Give **one** reason why Holy Week is a time of significance in the world religion
   you have ticked above.          (8 marks)

### 2007, HL, Section 2, Q2

This drawing is based on the Last Supper.

A. Pick one thing from the drawing which shows
   that this is the Last Supper.          (2 marks)

B. On which of the following days of the week did
   Jesus celebrate the Last Supper?- (Tick the
   correct box)          (2 marks)
   Wednesday  ☐  Thursday  ☐  Friday  ☐

## Questions *(Continued)*

C. Give two reasons why the Last Supper was important for the first Christians. (6 marks)

### Section 4 Question

### 2004, HL, Section 4, Q2

A. Write the name of each of the following seas in the spaces marked on the map (4 marks)

Dead Sea

Sea of Galilee

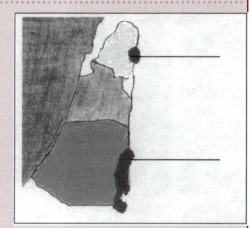

B. a. Outline the role of the Pharisees in the religious life of people in Palestine at the time of Jesus. (12 marks)

b. Describe **one** incident from the life of Jesus when he was in conflict with a Pharisee. (10 marks)

c. Imagine you are the Pharisee in this conflict. Outline your reason for opposing Jesus. (12 marks)

C. Tick **one** of the following characteristics of the kingdom of God and explain how it can be seen in an example of table fellowship from the life of Jesus: (12 marks)

Special place of the poor ☐ Love of neighbour ☐
Treatment of sinners and outcasts ☐

### Section 5 Questions

### 2004, HL, Section 5, Q2

Imagine you have been asked to give a talk at a Bible meeting explaining the stages involved in the development of the Gospels from the oral tradition to the written word. Outline the talk you would give making reference to the importance of the Gospels in the Christian community of faith.

### 2005, HL, Section 5, Q2

*In the parables Jesus tells people what the kingdom of God is like; in the miracles he shows people the kingdom of God among them.*
Outline what is revealed about the kingdom of God in one parable and one miracle you have studied.

●●●**Learning Objectives**

**In this chapter you will learn about:**

1   The origins and teachings of Islam, Judaism, Buddhism and Hinduism
2   The tradition, faith and practice today of Islam and Judaism

## 1 Islam

Make sure you know the following:

### Cultural context

### Points to note

**Cultural context** means how people lived in a particular place at a particular time.

- Islam began in Mecca, a place in what is today known as Saudi Arabia.
- At that time Mecca was a wealthy trading town. There was much corruption, drinking and gambling and also fighting between native tribes.
- There were some Christians and Jews living in Mecca but the majority of people were **polytheistic**.

- Mecca was a place of pilgrimage as a holy shrine, the **Kaaba**, was located there. People travelled to this building, thought to have been built by Abraham, to offer sacrifices and pray. Over time they began to worship idols and false Gods.

### Points to note

Polytheistic means believing in many Gods.

## The founder of Islam

### Points to note

A **founder** is a person who starts or sets up something.

- The founder of Islam was a man called **Muhammad**.
- Muhammad was born in Mecca in 570 CE. He was an orphan raised by his uncle. Although he could not read or write he became a respected businessman.
- At the age of twenty-five he married a widow named Khadijah.
- He became unhappy with the way people were living their lives in Mecca, so to find answers he went to a cave on Mt. Hira to pray.
- During the month known as **Ramadan** he received a revelation from God. The Angel Gabriel appeared to him and told him to read. Muhammad told the angel he could not read. After the angel told him 'read' three times he found that he could read.
- Amazed and frightened he went home and told his wife and she became the first **convert** to Islam.

### Points to note

A **convert** is someone who changes from one particular religion to another.

- Muhammad was a **prophet** which means a person called by God to receive an important message and preach it to the people.
- The angel continued to appear to Muhammad and said **Allah** had sent him. This is the name given to God in the Islamic faith.
- The religion became known as **Islam** and the followers were called **Muslims**.
- The powerful leaders in Mecca did not want Muhammad to preach his message as they wanted things to remain the way they were. Muhammad was telling the people to stop being corrupt and follow the one true God, Allah. Before long Muhammad and his followers began to be persecuted and tortured.
- In 622 CE the Muslims fled to a place called **Medina**. This event is known as the **Hijra** and marks the start of the Islamic calendar.

- In 629 CE Muhammad and his followers marched back into Mecca and removed all the idols from the Kaaba. It was once again a place of worship to the one true God, Allah.
- Muhammad died in 632 CE in Medina, where he is buried.

## Sources of evidence

- The main source of evidence is the **Qur'an**. Muslims believe it is the word of Allah told to Muhammad by the Angel Gabriel. It contains all their beliefs and moral codes.
- The Qur'an is made up of 114 chapters or surahs. It is written in Arabic. Many Muslims try to learn parts of it of by heart. It gives very detailed information on how Muslims should live their lives.
- **The Sunnah:** The Sunnah is a book formed from the Hadith. The Hadith is the traditions of Muhammad and contains details of his words and actions during his lifetime. Muslims see it as a role model for how they should live their lives.

## Islamic beliefs

The **Five Pillars of Faith** are the central **beliefs** of Islam.

### Points to note

**Beliefs** are core or central ideas of a religion, which give it its identity and often affects the lives of the believers.

1   **Shahadah (Creed):** 'There is only one God and Muhammad is his messenger.' All other beliefs come from this. Muslims say this before they pray and first thing in the morning and last thing at night.
2   **Salah (Prayer):** Muslims pray five times a day. The different elements involved in praying form a ritual. First Muslims must perform **wudu**. This is washing themselves in a certain way before praying. They also remove their shoes and pray on a prayer mat, kneeling on the ground. They must face in the direction of Mecca. Muslims then follow a set pattern of movements and say verses from the Qur'an to form a **ra'ka** or standard unit of prayer.
3   **Zakah (Charity):** Muslims give two and a half percent of their annual savings to the poor. It reminds Muslims to share the wealth Allah has given them. It is seen as a form of prayer and Muslims often give it during the month of Ramadan.
4   **Sawm (Fasting):** Fasting takes place during the month of Ramadan. Muslims also pray more during this time and read the Qur'an in order to try to lead better lives. During Ramadan Muslims eat a light breakfast before dawn and then a light meal after sunset. Elderly and sick people who are unable to fast will instead provide a meal for a poor person.

5 **Hajj (Pilgrimage):** Every Muslim should try to make the trip to Mecca, once in their lifetime, to perform the **Hajj**. It takes place during the twelfth month of the Islamic calendar. All Muslims come together dressed in white robes to show they are all equal and to pray to Allah. They begin by walking around the Kaaba seven times. Then they walk seven times between two hills to the well of Zam Zam where the Angel Gabriel appeared to Abraham's wife. After this they travel to Mina and camp for the night. The next day Muslims go to the Plain of Arafat and spend a day standing in prayer. The following day they return to Mina and throw stones at three pillars to symbolise their rejection of Satan. They offer an animal for sacrifice and give the meat to the poor. They then travel to Medina and pray at Muhammad's burial place. Finally they return to the Kaaba and circle it once more.

## Practices and ritual events

- **Birth:** When a Muslim baby is born the words of the Shahadah are whispered into their ear. After seven days a naming ceremony takes place. Muslim boys are circumcised.
- **Death:** After death a Muslim's body is washed, they are dressed in white robes and are buried as soon as possible on their right side facing the direction of Mecca.

## Festivals

Islam has two festivals called Eid al-Adha and Eid al-Fitr.

### Points to note

*REVISE WISE* *POINTS TO NOTE*

A **festival** is a special time set aside by a religion to celebrate a certain aspect of the religion, in a particular way.

| | Eid al-Adha | Eid al-Fitr |
|---|---|---|
| When | The day after Muslim pilgrims stop and pray on the Plain of Arafat, during the twelfth month of the Islamic calendar | The first day of the month of Shawal at the end of Ramadan |
| Why | It remembers Abraham's willingness to sacrifice his son for Allah. Allah accepted a lamb as a symbol of Abraham's devotion | It is used as an occasion to thank Allah for supporting Muslims during Ramadan. It is a joyful festival celebrated by all |

| Eid al-Adha | Eid al-Fitr |
|---|---|
| **How** There are early morning communal prayers. The Imam gives a sermon recalling the story of Abraham and his family. An animal is sacrificed as a symbol of the Muslim's obedience to Allah. The meat is shared between the family and the poor. The festival lasts for three days | There is early morning prayer in the Mosque. Everyone attends wearing their best clothes. Donations collected during Ramadan are given to the poor so that they can join in the celebrations. Families and friends visit each others' homes. Children are given gifts and sweets. The festival lasts for three days |

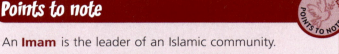

## Points to note

An **Imam** is the leader of an Islamic community.

## Place of worship

- The Islamic place of worship is called a **Mosque**.
- Mosques have no seats as space is needed to perform prayer movements. The floor is covered with carpet or prayer mats.
- Everyone removes their shoes before entering as a sign of respect and to keep the place of prayer clean.
- There are no statues or pictures as no one knows what Allah looks like. Instead there are mosaic patterns.
- There is a niche in the wall called a **mihrab** which shows the Muslims what direction Mecca is in so they know what way to face when praying.
- There is a pulpit for the Imam to lead the prayers.
- There are separate areas for men and women to pray.
- Muslims attend the Mosque on Fridays as it is their holy day.

## Islamic symbols

The crescent moon and star can be seen on the top of a Mosque. The moon symbolises the fact that Muslims follow a lunar calendar. The five points of the star represent the five pillars of Islam.

## Development and expansion

- The first followers of Islam suffered persecution and many fled to Abyssinia, known today as Ethiopia.

31

- After Muhammad died his close friend Abu Bakr became the first **caliph**. This means he was the chief Muslim civil and religious leader.
- The second caliph was called Omar. He was a great military leader and under his rule Islam spread to other countries such as Palestine and Egypt.
- Islamic travellers and merchants later brought their beliefs to places like France and Spain. People were impressed by what they heard about this new religion and began to convert to Islam.
- **Schism:** A schism means a split or a divide in a religion. After Muhammad's death there was a disagreement over leadership and the religion split into two groups called the **Shi'a** and **Sunni**. Shi'a is the smaller group and they believe that all leaders after Muhammad must be his direct descendants. The Sunni believe that the only true leadership is to be found in the Qur'an and how scholars interpret it.
- **Muslims in Ireland:** There has been a huge increase in the number of Muslims living in Ireland in the last ten years. There are somewhere between ten and twenty thousand. A large Mosque and cultural centre was built in Clonskeagh in Dublin to cater for the growing population. Some Muslims have come here from war-torn countries to seek refuge while others have come for education and employment.

## Tradition, faith and practice of Islam today

### Points to note

To **compare** two things means to look at what they have in common and the differences between them.

- Comparing Islam and Christianity, both are **monotheistic** faiths. Both believe in angels and life after death. They also have some of the same prophets such as Abraham and Moses. Prayer, fasting and charity are important parts of both religions.
- They are different as Christians see Jesus as the son of God whereas Muslims see him only as a great prophet. Islam does not accept the doctrine of the Trinity which is central to the Christian faith.

### Points to note

**Monotheistic** means a religion in which people believe in and worship only one god.

- **Lifestyle:** In Islam certain things are **haram,** which means forbidden. Alcohol is haram as are certain foods such as pork. A Muslim must eat food that is **halal**. Halal meat is slaughtered in a certain way. All the blood must be drained out of the animal and a prayer must be said before the animal is killed. Muslim women are expected to dress modestly. So a Muslim's everyday life is affected by their religion.
- **Community:** The leader of the community is the Imam. Any Muslim man can become an Imam as long as he leads a good life. Imams know the Qur'an very well and their main role is to lead the community in prayers and help them understand their faith better.
- **Dialogue:** There has been much dialogue between Christianity and Islam. They have come together at times of importance, such as the events of September 11th 2001 (9/11), to pray. They have also sent leaders to visit each other's place of worship.

# 2 Judaism

**Make sure you know the following:**

## Cultural context

- Judaism is the oldest monotheistic world religion. It is known as the parent religion of Christianity and Islam.
- Judaism began about 4,000 years ago in the land we now call Israel. At that time the people were known as **Hebrews**. They were a nomadic people, which meant they travelled from place to place and so were influenced by **polytheistic** beliefs.

## The founders of Judaism

- **Abram:** Abram and his wife Sarah lived in Haran. Abram believed there was only one God. When Abram was seventy-five, this God spoke to him. God made a **covenant** or special agreement with Abram. God asked Abram to leave his home and travel to a place called **Canaan**, which would become the **Promised Land** for the Hebrew people. In return God would give Abram and Sarah, who had no children, 'descendants as numerous as the stars in the sky.' All God asked was that Abram and the Hebrew people would remain faithful to him and follow his laws. Abram kept his promise and set off on the long journey. Sarah had a son called Isaac. When Isaac was a young boy Abram believed God wanted him to sacrifice his son to show his obedience. At the last minute God told him to stop and Abram sacrificed an animal instead. After this Abram became known as Abraham. He was seen as the **patriarch** or founding father of the Jewish religion. As a sign of the covenant between God and his people Jewish males are circumcised. This is where the foreskin of a boy's penis is removed.

### Points to note

**Abraham** means 'father of many nations'.

- **Moses:** In later years Abraham's descendants had to move to Egypt when a famine struck the land. They soon became the slaves of their cruel Egyptian masters who were called Pharaohs. Moses was a Jew who earned his living as a shepherd. One day he saw a bush on fire but it was not actually burning. Suddenly God spoke to him and told him to go and help the Jewish people. Moses was frightened but he set off to see the Pharaoh. Moses asked the Pharaoh to let the Jewish people go free and return to their promised land. The Pharaoh refused and God sent ten plagues on Egypt such as swarms of locusts that ruined the crops. The last and most terrible plague was an angel of death that would pass over every house in Egypt, killing the first born son. The Jews were told to sacrifice a lamb and smear the blood on their doors so that the angel would pass over their houses leaving them safe. After this plague the Pharaoh agreed to let the Jews go. But he then changed his mind and sent his armies after the Jews to bring them back. God parted the waters of the Red Sea, allowing the Jews to pass through safely. This event became known as the **Exodus** and is one of the most important moments in the history of the Jewish religion. After that, Moses travelled with his people to Mount Sinai where he received the Torah, which contained the **Ten Commandments**.

### Points to note

**Exodus** – when Moses led the Jewish slaves out of Egypt to Mount Sinai.

## Kings, prophets and exile

- The Jews or **Israelites,** as they became known, reached their Promised Land and settled in. However, they had to fight to keep foreign invaders away. They realised as long as they kept their promise to God he would help them.
- God sent them leaders called Judges. In 1020 BC they had their first king called King Saul. It was King Saul who helped to unite all the different tribes of Israel and make them stronger.
- The greatest king of Israel was King David. He made Jerusalem the capital city and his son King Solomon built the first temple there so that the people could worship their God.

- The kingdom eventually split in two, with Israel in the north and Judah in the south. The people began to forget their covenant with God and failed to follow the Ten Commandments. Once again God sent them help in the form of prophets.

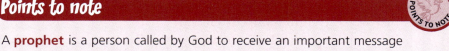

## Points to note

A **prophet** is a person called by God to receive an important message and preach it to the people.

- The prophets reminded the people to live good lives as God wanted them to. They warned them what would happen if they did not. Two of the most famous prophets were Jeremiah and Isaiah.
- In 586 BCE, in a battle, the temple in Jerusalem was destroyed and many Israelites were taken into slavery. They turned to God for help and knew they must return to the covenant.
- In time they returned home and built a new temple to thank their God. The laws given to them in the Torah became the most important thing for them. They even made new laws and their religious leaders became known as scribes or rabbis.
- In 63 BCE the Romans gained control of their land. In 70 CE their temple was destroyed again. The Jews began to leave their Promised Land and travel to places such as the Middle East and Europe taking their faith with them. They tried to remain God's chosen people, the people of the covenant.

## Points to note

A **rabbi** is a religious leader in the Jewish faith.

## Sources of evidence

The Jewish Bible is known in Hebrew as the **Tenakh**. It contains three books:

1  The **Torah** (Pentateuch)
2  The **Nevi'im** (Prophets)       } Tenakh
3  The **Ketuvim** (Holy Writings)

### The Torah

The Torah is the most important sacred text for Jewish people. It is made up of the first five books of the Old Testament. It tells the history of the Jewish people and their moral and legal codes.

### From oral to written tradition

- The history and beliefs were first passed down from generation to generation through the spoken word. It was later written down so that it would not be forgotten or changed. It was written mainly in Hebrew. If the Torah is being copied for use it must be written on scrolls. It is so sacred that it cannot be touched. The Torah contains the 613 mitzvot or rules that were given to Moses by God.
- To help people understand the writings in the Torah the **Oral Torah** or Law came about. These include the **Mishnah**, which gives instructions on issues such as legal matters and marriage. Important rabbis and scholars wrote it. The **Talmud** is another text that helps people to understand how to apply the old laws to new problems.

## Jewish beliefs

The Jewish people's main beliefs can be summed up as follows:

1  **Monotheism:** There is one almighty, powerful God.
2  **Identity:** The Jews believe that they are God's chosen people.
3  **Covenant:** Jews must remain true to the covenant made with God through Abraham and Moses.

These beliefs are often remembered by the people through **rites** and **rituals**.

### Points to note

**Rites** and **rituals** are words or actions that are performed by Jews in a special way at a certain time.

## Practices and ritual events

The best way to understand the rites and rituals of Judaism is to follow the life of a typical Jewish person from their birth to their death.

**Birth**: Eight days after a baby boy is born the **Covenant of Circumcision** takes place. It is a sign that the person is entering into the same covenant with God, as Abraham did. The baby is brought to the synagogue, the Jewish place of worship, where his father says a special blessing over him. He is given a

Hebrew name as well as an English one. Afterwards there is a party. Baby girls have a special naming ceremony.

**Adulthood**: At thirteen years old a Jewish boy is seen as an adult in his religion. A **Bar Mitzvah** takes place. It means 'son of the commandment'. The boy studies hard in preparation. He wears the tallit, which is a prayer robe or shawl. He also wears the tefillin, which are two leather boxes containing biblical verses worn on the head and arm. He goes to the synagogue and is called up to read from the Torah in Hebrew. His father gives him a blessing and afterwards there is a party for family and friends. Girls celebrate a **Bat Mitzvah**, which means 'daughter of the commandment'.

**Marriage**: Jews see marriage as **Kiddushin**, which means 'holy'. The man signs a contract beforehand in which he promises to take care of his wife. The ceremony takes place in the synagogue under a **huppah** or canopy. It is a symbol of the couple's home. Seven blessings are said or sung. The bride and groom take a sip of wine from the same glass. The man then places a ring on the woman's finger and reads the promises from the contract. He then takes the wine glass and wraps it in a cloth, puts it on the floor and stamps on it. This is to symbolise the destruction of the temple. It reminds everyone that life is fragile. All the guests shout, 'Mazal Tov', which means 'Good Luck'.

**Death**: There are **three** stages of mourning when a Jewish person dies. The funeral takes place within 24 hours of the death so that the grieving can begin. Jewish people believe in expressing their feelings. The family make small tears in their clothes as a sign of their grief. The body is washed and wrapped in a plain linen shroud. After a few prayers and a speech the burial takes place. A special prayer of mourning called the **Kaddish** is said. For the next week the family of the deceased sit **shiva**, which means seven. Friends and family come to the house to mourn and help the family in any way they can. For the next month there is **sheloshim**, which means thirty. The male members of the family visit the synagogue every day. The third stage is **yahrzeit**, which means year time. The gravestone is erected, a special candle is lit and prayers are said for the deceased.

## Festivals and special times

All religions have special times that are set apart as different. These are known as sacred times. This means they are holy. Three of the most important festivals in Judaism are: Passover, Hanukkah and Yom Kippur.

|  | Passover | Hanukkah | Yom Kippur |
|---|---|---|---|
| When | One week in the spring | Eight days in December | One day in September |
| Why | To celebrate the Israelites' escape from slavery in Egypt at the time of Moses | To celebrate the victory over enemies who had made the temple unclean by bringing in idols. Temple lights were relit and the temple was fit again for worship | A time of repentance. The high priest prays to God to ask him to forgive the sins of the people |
| How | Families have a seder meal at which the story of the Exodus is read. Certain foods are eaten which represent parts of the story, e.g. bitter herbs recall the bitterness of slavery | One candle is lit each day until all eight are lighting together. Special foods are eaten and gifts are exchanged | For 10 days people think about what they have done wrong in the past year. Then they fast for 25 hours and go to the synagogue to pray for forgiveness |

## Prayer and practice

- Jews can pray anywhere and at any time. One of the most important times of prayer is at the weekend and it takes place in the family home and in the synagogue.
- **Shabbat (Jewish Sabbath):** This time of rest and prayer begins on a Friday evening at sunset and ends at the same time the following day. It is celebrated because the Torah says that after God's work of creation he rested. The Jewish people use this day to remember their God. The family is central to the celebration. Before it begins the family clean the house and prepare the food so that they have no work to do on the actual day. The mother of the family lights two candles and says a special prayer to begin. The father then blesses the children and says the Kiddush blessing over a cup of wine. Songs are sung between the different courses. On Saturday morning there is a service in the synagogue. When Shabbat is over on Saturday evening a candle is lit and a box of sweet spices is passed around as a symbol of hope for good things to come in the following week.
- Prayer also takes place in the synagogue and Jews are required to attend whenever possible. There are three services a day. The services are short.

The **Shema**, which is the most important prayer in Judaism, is read. The Torah is also read. There must be ten adult males present for a service to take place. Any male over thirteen years old can lead the service as long as he can read Hebrew.

- **Tallit:** A prayer robe or shawl with knotted tassels worn by most Jewish males when they pray.
- **Kippah:** A cap that Jews wear for prayer. Orthodox Jews wear one all the time.
- **Tefillin:** Small leather boxes that contain tiny scrolls with the Shema prayer written on them. They are worn on the head or arm.
- **Kosher food:** The word kosher means clean and pure. Rules about kosher food come from the Torah. Pork and shellfish are not kosher and so must not be eaten. Kosher meat must be slaughtered in a certain way. Meat and dairy products must not be eaten together.

## Place of worship

- The Jewish place of worship is called a **synagogue**. Jews use it as a place not only for worship but also for office work, parties, study and meetings.
- Every synagogue has a cupboard called the **ark**, which is behind a curtain. In it are the scrolls of the Torah.
- Above the ark is the **Ner Tamid**. This is a perpetual light, a sign of the everlasting covenant.
- Above the ark are two tablets or plaques. They represent the tablets of stone on which the Ten Commandments were given to Moses by God.
- In the centre of the synagogue is the **bimah**. This is a raised platform from which the Torah and prayers are read.
- **The Western** or **Wailing Wall:** The Western or Wailing Wall in Jerusalem is a place of pilgrimage for Jewish people. The Jewish people began to worship their God in the Temple built in the time of King David. The Ark of the Covenant was kept there, which contained the two tablets of stone bearing the Ten Commandments that God gave to Moses. After the Romans destroyed it in 70 AD all that was left was the Western Wall of the building. Jews go to this site today to pray. Some write their prayers on little bits of paper and stick them in the cracks in the wall. Other Jewish people can be overcome with grief at the wall as they remember the persecution their people have suffered over the centuries. This is why it is also known as the Wailing Wall.

## Jewish symbols

- **The menorah:** A seven- or nine-branched candlestick. Light is often used in religions as a symbol of hope and comfort.
- **The Star of David:** Found in synagogues. Some Jewish people wear it as a sign of pride in their faith. It remembers the great King of Israel, King David.

- **The Mezuzah:** A small case that holds a scroll on which the Shema is written. Most Jewish homes have them attached to the door frames in the house. Jews will often touch the Mezuzah, and then kiss their fingers as they pass it as a sign of love for what the writing means.

## Persecution and expansion of Judaism

- The Jewish religion has a very troubled history, for example their time in slavery in Egypt and being ruled by foreign invaders such as the Romans. Jews also suffered persecution because of their religious beliefs later in history.
- After the Jews left Israel in 70 CE they went to places such as North Africa in an event known as the **diaspora**.

### Points to note

**Diaspora** means the scattering of the Jews from Israel after it was taken over by the Romans in 70 CE.

- In 1290 Jews were expelled from England and only allowed back in the seventeenth century.
- In the 1880s they were forced out of Russia and many went to America.
- The worst period of persecution was between 1933 and 1945 in Europe at the hands of Hitler and the Nazis. In an event known as the **Holocaust**, their homes and businesses were destroyed; they were banned from public places and were sent to concentration camps. Millions died in gas chambers.
- **Schism:** A schism is a split or a divide in a religion. Two of the largest branches of the Jewish religion are Orthodox and Reform Judaism. Orthodox Jews are very traditional and follow the Torah very closely. Reform Jews do not follow the same strict laws. They adapt the laws of the Torah to suit life in modern times.
- There are thought to be approximately 14 million Jewish people in the world today. This is a small number compared to other world religions; this is due to the fact that so many Jews were lost during the holocaust.
- Jews have been living in Ireland since 1079. They have played a big part in Irish business and politics over the years. In 1988 there was a Jewish Lord Mayor of Dublin.

## Tradition, faith and practice of Judaism today

- Jewish leaders are called **rabbis**. They are most importantly teachers. They study the Torah closely and advise the people on how to apply it to their lives. They also lead synagogue services. They are very involved in the community and are respected by all members.

● Education is very important to Jews. Synagogues are places of learning as well as worship. Children attend classes in Hebrew from a young age.

## Points to note

To **compare** two things means to look at what they have in common and the differences between them.

● Comparing Judaism and Christianity, both are **monotheistic** religions, both follow the Ten Commandments and both have meals as part of their worship. Some of the differences between them are that Jewish people are still waiting for a Messiah to arrive whereas Christians believe he arrived in Jesus Christ. Christians celebrate their holy day on Sunday while the Jewish holy day starts on Friday and ends on Saturday night.

● **Dialogue:** Judaism and Catholicism did not always get along but the Second Vatican Council reminded Catholics to embrace and respect other religions. This was highlighted in 1986 when Pope John Paul II visited a synagogue in Rome. The Council of Jews and Christians was set up to improve relations between the two religions.

# 3 Hinduism

**Make sure you know the following:**

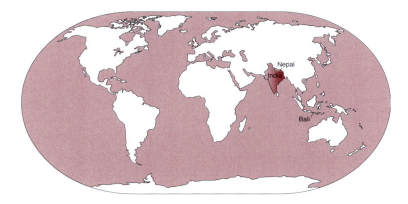

## Cultural context

● Hinduism is one of the oldest world religions.
● There are approximately 900 million followers of the Hindu religion today.
● It is the predominant religion in Nepal and Bali.

## Founder of Hinduism

Hinduism has no founder.

## Hindu beliefs

- The main emphasis of Hinduism is on a way of living rather than on a way of thought.
- Hindus believe in a supreme soul or spirit that has no shape or form. This is called the **Brahman** and everything in the universe flows from this.
- There are many Hindu Gods and Goddesses but there are **three** important Gods:
  - Brahma.
  - Vishnu.
  - Shiva.
- Hindus believe that they must always do what is right and correct for themselves – this is called **dharma**.
- Hindus believe that when you die, your soul is reborn in another body as an animal or a person. This cycle of birth and rebirth is called **Samsara**.
- Hindus believe that you are reborn over and over until you are perfect. Because of this they believe that when you do good, good will come your way, and if you do bad, bad will follow you. This is called **Karma**.

## Sources of evidence

- Hindus have no sacred text but they have many holy books.
- The oldest Hindu sacred texts are from the four collections of prayers, hymns and magic spells called **Vedas**. They teach and guide Hindus on how they should live their lives.

## Practices and ritual events

Rites of passage are different ceremonies that take place to mark important events.

1   **Baptism:** Soon after the baby is born into a Hindu family a prayer is whispered into its ear by someone in the family. This is a prayer of thanksgiving. When the family are gathered together the father dips his gold pen in honey and writes the word 'aum' on the baby's tongue. The baby's hair is then cut symbolising that any badness in a previous life will not affect this life. Twelve days after the baby is born they are named at a naming ceremony. This is done in the presence of the family members and the **Brahmin** priest.

2   **Marriage:** Arranged marriages are common to Hindu people. The marriage ceremony is held in the girl's home place or temple. A marriage is a very happy occasion. Marriage is a sacred ritual in Hinduism. The celebrations may last two or three days with all wedding gifts displayed.

## Points to note

An **arranged marriage** means that the parents plan for their children to marry someone that they choose to be suitable.

3   **Death:** When a Hindu dies, the body is washed and then anointed with oil. It is carried to a funeral pyre to be cremated. The ashes are gathered and then scattered in a nearby river. If a family is planning a pilgrimage to the **River Ganges** they may decide to keep the ashes safe until that time. The waters of the River Ganges are believed to be sacred.

## Festivals and sacred times

- A religious festival is a special time usually remembered by fasting or celebration. They are times of music, dancing, stories and food. The most popular festivals are: **Holi, Divali** and **Khumbh Mela**.
- **The Sacred Thread Ceremony:** At this ceremony the boy seeks spiritual identity. He accepts a spiritual teacher as a father and the Vedas as a mother. He receives a sacred thread which is usually worn throughout his lifetime. He shaves his head for the ceremony. He is given a spiritual name to symbolise his 'second birth'.  After that the thread is wrapped around the thumb of his right hand and a prayer is chanted at dawn, noon and dusk. He takes a vow to study the Vedas and serve his teachers.
- **Pilgrimage to the River Ganges:** The River Ganges is located in the city of Varanasi. Pilgrims bring flowers with them to the river and many bathe in the river to help cleanse them of any wrong-doing. Often the ashes of a loved one are scattered at the river. These pilgrimages to the River Ganges are considered to be a family time.

## Place of worship

- To **worship** something is to show adoration and respect.
- The Hindu word for worship is **puja**.
- Hindus often worship in their homes. They chant over and over the sacred word 'aum'.
- Hindus also worship in **temples.** There are no seats in the temples. The shrine room is called the **Garbagriha**. A canopy covers the Garbagriha. The priest looks after this area by dressing the statue in colourful robes and garlands before puja. People take off their shoes and women cover their heads. Together, people chant verses from the holy books.

**Hindus believe there are five sacred duties:**

1   To perform puja or worship.
2   To say aloud parts of the scriptures.

43

3  To respect their parents and older people.

4  To give food and shelter to those who are lost.

5  To feed and care for their animals, especially the cow. In India, the cow is regarded as a sacred animal. It is worshipped for its life-giving qualities. It provides milk for food, leather to sell and droppings for fuel. Hindus are vegetarians because they do not believe in killing a creature as it is no different to them.

### Hindu prayer life

1  Prayer to many world religions is conversation with God.

2  Hindu prayer is different as it involves repeating a name for the Brahman over and over.

3  It is done using a mantra which is a phrase that Hindus use over and over during **meditation**. This mantra is given to a Hindu for his or her lifetime by a spiritual **guru**.

## Points to note

A **guru** is a spiritual adviser in Hinduism.

*REVISE WISE*
*POINTS TO NOTE*

4  Prayer is a personal thing to each Hindu as they worship a lot in their homes and only gather in the temple for holy days. Even while together in the temple, they pray alone.

5  Meditation is one way that Hindus pray.

## Mahatma Gandhi – a disciple of the faith

Mohandas Gandhi was born in North West India in 1869. After his marriage he left India and went to London to study law. While in London he remained loyal to his Hindu beliefs and began to read sacred writings. The **Bhagavad-Gita** (an important Hindu text) had a strong impact on his life and he began to cut down on his daily expenses, walking everywhere and eating less.

After qualification as a barrister he accepted a job with an Indian law firm in South Africa and moved there with his family. He experienced at first hand the life of Indian people in South Africa. He was once thrown off a train, even though his ticket was valid, as he was not sitting in the right carriage. The turning point in his life came when he refused to give his seat to a white person on a stage coach and was beaten by the driver.

From this point he committed himself to defending his dignity as an Indian and as a human being. He encouraged the Indian population to challenge the conditions they were living under. He developed a method of direct social action called **Satyagraha,** which was based on the principles of courage, truth and non-violence. Ghandi was arrested many times in both South Africa and India, but he believed it was an honourable thing to do to go to prison for a just cause.

Later he returned to India where he campaigned for India's independence from Great Britain. In 1947, India gained its independence from Great Britain. However Gandhi's dream of a united India where Muslims and Hindus could live together in peace did not happen. Divisions between Muslims and Hindus resulted in the later partition of India and Pakistan. Ghandi saw the partition of India as a tragedy.

## Hindu symbols

Many Hindu symbols include the notion of inner purity. Some of these symbols include:

- 'Aum' – a mantra chanted at the beginning of prayers and rituals.
- Bindi – a coloured dot worn on the forehead of women to symbolise female energy.
- The cow – which represents life for Hindus.

## Tradition, faith and practice of Hinduism today

Comparing Hinduism and Christianity, both encourage believers to treat others as they would like to be treated themselves.

# 4 Buddhism

Make sure you know the following:

## Cultural context

The Buddhist religion is an offshoot of Hinduism. It began in the north of India around the fifth century BCE.

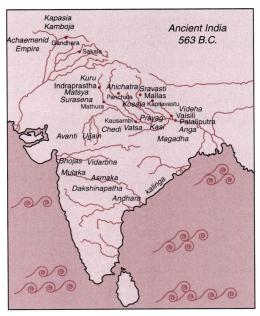

## The founder of Buddhism

**Siddhartha Gautama** was the founder of Buddhism.

- Siddhartha Gautama was the son of a king and queen in the border area between India and Nepal.
- At his birth a wise man prophesised that he would become a great ruler one day.
- He was shielded from the outside world as he lived in great splendour inside a castle.
- One day he decided to leave the castle and see what the outside world was really like. This journey affected him greatly and it changed his life.
- He saw poverty and sickness for the first time. He met a monk who had no possessions but was still content with life. From that moment on he vowed that his life would be like that of the monks.
- He began his life of prayer and fasting but he found there were no real answers to the questions he sought, so he decided to move on while still searching. Many years passed and no answers came.
- One day as he sat under a tree in Bodh Gaya in India he closed his eyes and began to meditate. He felt something inside and when he opened his eyes, he knew that he had found the truth and a way out from the suffering around him.
- His enlightenment showed him that people suffered because they were never happy with what they had, and always strived for more things in life.
- People needed to learn a way of thinking and behaving – his theory the **'Middle Way'** describes a life lived somewhere between poverty and luxury.
- He set out to describe the Four Noble Truths which states that life is full of suffering and the cause of suffering is greed.
- The only way to end this is the 'Middle Way' which finds happiness between extreme luxury and poverty.
- He returned to the monks with his findings. They were impressed with his ideas and became his first followers.
- The monks named him **Buddha** which means 'Enlightened One'.

## Sources of evidence

There are many sacred writings that belong to the Buddhist faith. The Buddha was a great teacher but he never wrote anything down. After his death his teachings were passed on by word of mouth. Some were later written down by his followers and include the teachings called **Tripitaka** which are followed by Theravada Buddhists in southern Asia. Tripitaka means 'three baskets'. Within each basket there is an important teaching.

1   **The Vinaya:** Discipline involving rules for monks and nuns on how to live like the Buddha.
2   **The Abhidhamma:** The main teachings of the Four Noble Truths and the Middle Way.
3   **The Sutra:** An explanation of the Buddha's teaching and the way of looking at life.

## Buddhist beliefs

A **creed** is a religious belief that sums up what the followers believe in and live by. The Buddha told his followers to achieve a state of **nirvana**, which is a state of perfect happiness and peace. He believed this could be achieved by the following:

- The Four Noble Truths.
- The Eightfold Path.
- The Five Precepts.

### The Four Noble Truths

The most important Buddhist beliefs/truths are found in the sacred text called the Four Noble Truths. The truths are:

- **Duktha:** There is no such thing as permanent happiness because even the happiest of moments come to an end.
- **Samudaya:** The main cause of our suffering is desire and greed.
- **Nirvana:** Suffering can be brought to an end. We can find true happiness and peace by not being greedy.
- **Magga:** The Middle Way is the path to true happiness. There are eight steps on this journey and it is the solution to suffering.

It is only by believing that other people suffer that we can come to terms with our daily struggles and difficulties. This is what is taught through the Duktha and Samudaya. It is developed further in the Magga which has eight parts to it.

### The Eightfold Path

The Middle Way is the Buddhist way of life. Each of the eight steps must be followed.

1   Right understanding.
2   Right thought.
3   Right speech.
4   Right action.
5   Right livelihood.
6   Right effort.
7   Right mindfulness.
8   Right concentration.

The Eightfold Path can be divided into three sections: wisdom, morality and meditation.

### The Five Precepts

The Five Precepts are like the Ten Commandments. They help Buddhists stay true to their faith. They emphasise respect for life. These five rules help Buddhists stay true to life.

1  One should not kill another living creature.
2  One should not steal from another.
3  One should not misuse the physical senses.
4  One should not tell lies to others.
5  One should not take drink or drugs.

## Practices and ritual events

### Meditation

- Buddhists chant and meditate in silence while worshipping.
- Meditation is a communal type of prayer, one that helps free the mind.
- It can be done by oneself but is best done in a group under the guidance of a leader.
- Some Buddhists have a mantra (repeating chant) that helps them to concentrate.

### Rites of passage

- A ceremony is a formal religious or public occasion celebrating an event.
- There are a number of ritual events in Buddhism that involve ceremonies.
- Three Buddhist ceremonies are: birth, marriage and death.
- **Birth:** When a baby enters the world they are brought to the temple for the naming ceremony. Water, candles and wax are used in this ceremony. Through fire, water and air the child has harmony in their lives.
- **Marriage:** Buddhists have no wedding ceremony. It is not a religious event, but when the marriage is registered a lot of Buddhist couples go to the temple to receive a blessing. Families gather together to celebrate the event.
- **Death:** Buddhists do not fear death. Death is a celebratory time for Buddhists as it releases one from suffering. A body can be cremated or buried.

## Place of worship

- Buddhists worship in holy places called temples.
- They do not worship in a community environment.
- They do not need other people to help them worship.
- Images of the Buddha are found in homes and Buddhist temples.

- The Stupa (monument) preserves and enshrines the relic (something that is holy) of the Buddha in the temple.
- Buddhists honour what the statue represents.

### Sacred places

- A pilgrimage is a journey to a holy place to pray and honour someone.
- Buddhists go on pilgrimages to honour their founder and important stages in his life: his birth, enlightenment, first sermon to monks and his death.
- Many Buddhists make a pilgrimage to Bodh Gaya in India where Siddhartha achieved enlightenment.

### Buddhist festivals

- A festival is a time of celebration for all involved.
- Two important Buddhist festivals celebrated are Vesak/Wesak and Vassa.
- The Buddha recommended to his followers that if they were to get on they should 'meet together regularly in large numbers.'
- Festivals are important to the Buddhist community as they show devotion and gratitude to the Buddha and his teachings.

## Buddhist symbols

The Lotus plant is an important symbol to Buddhists.

## Development and expansion of Buddhism

As Buddhism spread from India to other countries it adapted itself to the needs of individual cultures. Buddhism has experienced a huge revival in the last thirty-five years. Today there are about 350 million Buddhists worldwide.

## Sample Question and Answer

Here are three sample Higher Level questions and answers from Section 5 of the examination paper.

### 2007, HL, Section 5, Q3

Buddhism    Hinduism    Islam    Judaism

Describe a time of the year that is important for members in one of the above world religions.                    (70 marks)

In your answer you should explain why that time of year is important for followers today.

## Sample Question and Answer (Continued)

A time of year that is important for followers of the Islamic religion is the Hajj. This is a pilgrimage that Muslims make to Mecca during the twelfth month of the Islamic calendar. It is one of the five Pillars of Faith for Muslims and all Muslims should try to make the journey at least once in their lifetime.

Muslims journey to Mecca from all around the world. They make the pilgrimage dressed in plain white robes to show that they are all equal before Allah. They begin at the Kaaba and walk around it seven times. Then they walk between two hills just as Abraham's wife did when she was searching for water. This is called the well of Zam Zam. After this they travel to Mina. The following day they spend the whole day standing in prayer on the Plain of Arafat. Then they return to Mecca and collect pebbles along the way. They use these pebbles the next day to throw at stone pillars that represent the devil. A sacrifice then takes place. They then go to Medina and pray at Muhammad's burial place. Finally they go back to Mecca and circle the Kaaba again.

The reason why this time of year is so important is because it gives Muslims a chance to meet and pray with other believers. It also shows their devotion to Allah. They get to remember important people, times and places associated with their religion. There is even a festival to celebrate the event called Eid al-Adha.

## Sample Question and Answer

Tick one of the following world religions that you have studied:
Buddhism ☐ Christianity ☐ Islam ☐ Judaism ☐ Hinduism ☐

Imagine that you have been asked to compile a fact file on your chosen religion. Write about your chosen religion under two of the following headings:

Key beliefs     Sacred places     Sacred times     Sacred texts

The world religion that I am answering on is **HINDUISM**.

### Sacred Places

The *River Ganges* is a sacred place for Hindus. It is in the city of Varanasi. Many Hindus gather there to bathe in the water to help cleanse them of any wrongdoing. Often when a person dies their ashes are scattered in the river. There are steps along the river bank where pilgrims stand holding flowers.

## Sample Question and Answer (*Continued*)

**Sacred Texts**

*Hindus have no one sacred text. They have many holy books. The oldest sacred texts are from the four collections of prayers, hymns and magic spells called the Vedas. They were put together about 3,000 years ago and they teach and guide Hindus on how they should live their lives. One other important text is called the Upanishads which are teachings presented in the form of stories and parables told by teachers to their students.*

B. Imagine that as part of the fact file you have been asked to compare this world religion with another of your choice. Identify the similarities in the space provided below.

*The religion I am comparing Hinduism to is Buddhism.*

- *Both religions are polytheistic religions which means they believe in more that one God.*
- *Buddhism in an offshoot of Hinduism.*
- *Both religions use meditation as a type of prayer.*
- *The temple is an important place to both religions.*
- *There is a common belief to treat all people with respect and dignity.*

## Sample Question and Answer

You have been asked to introduce a world religion to fifteen-year-old students who are interested in learning about it. Pick **one** of the following and answer the questions below:

Buddhism    Hinduism    Islam    Judaism

Name of world religion: *Judaism*

A. The students are interested in religious festivals. Write a description of **two** festivals in this religion describing when, how and why these festivals are celebrated.

i. Name of festival: *Passover*

a. When is this festival celebrated?

*This festival is celebrated for one week in the spring.*

b. How is this festival celebrated?

*Jewish families have a Seder meal at which the story of the Exodus is read. Certain foods such as bitter herbs are eaten to represent parts of the story.*

c. Why is this festival celebrated?

*Passover is celebrated to remember and celebrate the Israelites' escape from slavery in Egypt at the time of Moses.*

## Sample Question and Answer *(Continued)*

ii. Name of festival: *Hanukkah*

a. When is this festival celebrated?

*This festival is celebrated for eight days in December.*

b. How is this festival celebrated?

*One candle is lit each day until all eight are lighting together. Special foods are eaten and gifts are exchanged.*

c. Why is this festival celebrated?

*It celebrates the victory over enemies who had made the Temple unclean. Temple lights were relit and the temple was fit again for worship.*

B. Describe in detail another aspect of the lifestyle of believers in this world religion that you would regard as important.

*Another aspect of the lifestyle of Jews that is important is their weekly Sabbath. It begins of Friday evening and ends on Saturday evening. It is a holy day for rest and prayer. The house is cleaned before it begins. The mother lights two candles and says a special prayer to begin. Then the father blesses the children and says the blessing. There is special bread and songs between the different courses. On Saturday morning there is a service in the synagogue. On Saturday evening when the Shabbat is over, a special candle is lit and sweet spices are given out. Everyone wishes each other a good week.*

## Questions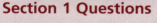

### Section 1 Questions
### 2003, HL, Section 1, Q7

Read the lists of sacred texts and world religions given below. **One** sacred text has been matched to the religion with which it is associated as an example for you. Make **one** other match. (5 marks)

**Example**: Gospel
**Answer:** Christianity

| Sacred Texts | Religions |
| --- | --- |
| Vedas | Buddhism |
| Hebrew | Christianity |
| Qur'an | Hinduism |
| Tripitaka | Islam |
| Gospel | Judaism |

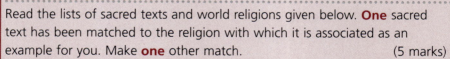

## Questions *(Continued)*

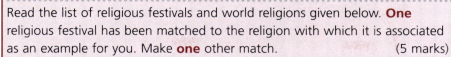

### 2004, HL, Section 1, Q3

Read the list of religious festivals and world religions given below. **One** religious festival has been matched to the religion with which it is associated as an example for you. Make **one** other match. (5 marks)

**Example**: Christmas
**Answer:** Christianity

| Religious Festivals | Religions |
| --- | --- |
| Christmas | Buddhism |
| Eid-al Adha | Christianity |
| Holi | Hinduism |
| Rosh Hashanah | Islam |
| Sangha Day | Judaism |

### 2005, HL, Section 1, Q7

Read the lists of leaders and world religions given below. **One** leader has been matched to the religion with which he is most associated as an example for you. Make **one** other match. (5 marks)

**Example**: Jesus
**Answer:** Christianity

| Leaders | Religions |
| --- | --- |
| Brahmins | Buddhism |
| Jesus | Christianity |
| King David | Hinduism |
| Muhammad | Islam |
| Siddhartha Gautama | Judaism |

### 2006, HL, Section 1, Q3

Read the list of religious symbols and the list of world religions given below. **One** religious symbol has been matched to the religion with which it is associated as an example for you. Make **one** other match. (5 marks)

**Example:** Cross
**Answer:** Christianity

| Religious Symbols | Religions |
| --- | --- |
| Aum | Buddhism |
| Menorah | Hinduism |
| Mihrab | Christianity |
| Prayer Wheel | Islam |
| Cross | Judaism |

### 2007, HL, Section 1, Q4

The title 'Rabbi' is most associated with a leader in which of the following world religions? (Tick the correct box) (5 marks)

Buddhism ☐  Hinduism ☐  Judaism ☐

## Questions *(Continued)*

### Section 4 Questions
### 2004, HL, Section 4, Q3

A. a. Tick **one** of the following world religions you have studied:

Buddhism  ☐    Hinduism  ☐    Islam  ☐    Judaism  ☐

Tick **one** country on the map below where the world religion you have chosen began.                                                                 (4 marks)

   b. Briefly describe **one** thing about the way people lived in the country
      you have chosen at the time this world religion began.        (10 marks)

B. a. Tick the creed or moral code listed below that is associated with your
      chosen world religion.                                        (8 marks)

   The Ten Commandments     ☐      The Five Pillars     ☐
   The Law of Karma         ☐      The Eightfold Path   ☐

   b. Outline **three** rules/guidelines from the creed or moral code you have
      ticked.                                                       (12 marks)

### 2005, HL, Section 4, Q3

A. Every religion has ideas about God, the world, humanity – ideas that
   shape the beliefs and rituals of that religion.

   a. State a key belief about God from one of the following world
      religions:                                                    (8 marks)

   Buddhism              Hinduism              Islam              Judaism

   World religion _____

   Key belief about God _____

   b. Describe how their belief about God influences the way of life of
      followers of this world religion today.                       (10 marks)

## Questions *(Continued)*

c. Outline how the life of an important person in the story of this world religion was influenced by his/her beliefs about God. (15 marks)

B. a. Name a religious ritual associated with one of the following world religions: (5 marks)

Buddhism          Hinduism          Islam          Judaism

World religion _____

Religious ritual _____

b. Explain the meaning of this ritual. (12 marks)

## 2006, HL, Section 4, Q3

A. a. Tick **one** of the following world religions you have studied and name the sacred text associated with it: (5 marks)

Buddhism ☐          Hinduism ☐          Islam ☐          Judaism ☐

Name of sacred text _____

b. Briefly explain why this sacred text is a document of faith. (10 marks)

B. a. Outline **one** religious ceremony in which the sacred text you have named above is used. (10 marks)

b. Describe **two** ways in which this sacred text influences the way of life of a follower of this world religion. (10 marks)

C. Buddhism          Hinduism          Islam          Judaism

Briefly describe a time of growth and development in one of the above world religions. (15 marks)

## 2007, HL, Section 4, Q3

A. Buddhism ☐          Hinduism ☐          Islam ☐          Judaism ☐

Tick **one** of the world religions above that you have studied.

a. Name **one** key person/group of people associated with the founding story of the world religion you have ticked above _____ (5 marks)

b. Explain why the person/group of people you have named is important in the founding story of the world religion you have ticked above. (10 marks)

B. Outline **one** way in which the story of the earliest followers influences members today in the world religion you have ticked above. (15 marks)

C. Explain how the world religion you have ticked above is linked to another major world religion. (20 marks)

## Questions *(Continued)*

### Section 5 Questions

### 2004, HL, Section 5, Q3

A.  Tradition can be described as a long established belief or custom. Describe **one** tradition that is popular in **one** of the following world religions that you have studied. Explain its origins and its significance for followers today. (70 marks)

Buddhism                    Hinduism                    Islam                    Judaism

### 2007, HL, Section 5, Q5

Ritual can help people to express their faith.

Discuss the importance of ritual for members of **one** of the following major world religions: (70 marks)

Buddhism            Christianity            Hinduism            Islam            Judaism

## Your revision notes

# Section D: The Question of Faith

## ●●● Learning Objectives

**In this chapter you will learn about:**
1 The situation of faith today
2 The beginning of faith in the asking of questions and the search for answers
3 The expressions of human questioning in modern culture
4 The characteristics of religious faith
5 The challenges to religious faith today

## 1 The Situation of Faith Today

Make sure you know the following:

- **Religious belief** means the things we believe to be true about God and the **faith** that we belong to.
- **Religious practice** is how we show these religious beliefs. It means putting what we believe about God and our faith into practice in our lives.
- The main changes that have taken place in religious belief and practice in Ireland in the last sixty years include:

  1 In the past religious statues and pictures were much more prominent in people's homes.
  2 Weekly routines revolved around religious events such as Benediction, Sunday mass, confession and Stations of the Cross.
  3 Most people did not eat meat on Fridays and fasted before Communion.
  4 The Angelus and the Rosary were said daily by most people.

## Changes and differences

1 In 1054 a **schism** or **split** occurred in the Christian Church. This resulted in the Catholic Church in the West and the Orthodox Church in the East.
2 **Politics** affected people's religious faith in Europe. World War II saw a huge number of the Jewish population being wiped out at the hands of Hitler in Nazi Germany. Communism made it difficult for people to practice their faith. The fall of the Berlin Wall in 1989 changed things once again and people began to express their faith more freely.
3 **Second Vatican Council (Vatican II):** This was a large church council that took place in the 1960s. The aim of Vatican II was to work for unity

among Christians and to encourage its members to work for justice and peace in the world. It also wanted to bring the church into the modern world. Practical changes it brought about included saying the mass in the language of the people (vernacular) instead of Latin. The priest also faced the people when celebrating mass instead of having his back to them. It also encouraged lay people to become more involved by allowing them to become Ministers of the Eucharist.

4  **Modernity** has seen a drop in the number of people actively participating in their churches. In 1981 83% of Catholics in Europe went to mass once a week or more. By 1999 that number dropped to 59%. However, more people said they believed in God. Possible reasons why people are not practicing their faith as much include:

- **Lifestyle:** People have busier lives and may not have the time or energy. There are more opportunities for leisure activities and shopping.
- **Freedom:** People have more freedom in a more liberal and free thinking society.
- **Church influence:** The Church does not have the same influence over people's lives.
- **Media:** The media has opened up new ideas and opinions to people.

5  **Vocations**: Numbers joining the priesthood dropped from 137 in 1980 to 49 in 1999. Possible reasons for the decline may be:
- There are more opportunities in education and employment for young people.
- A more materialistic world means people are more concerned with possessions and want jobs with high salaries and better benefits.
- Public opinion means that people may be less inclined to dedicate their lives to God and the Church because of what their peers might think.

## The bigger picture

Despite the above trends people still view religion as a major part of their lives' especially at times such as birth, marriage and death. They also turn to their faith at important moments as was seen at times such as 9/11 and the death of Pope John Paul II.

## Faith and practice in the life of the adolescent

Family, friends and the media are some of the biggest influences on the faith of teenagers. These influences can be both positive and negative.

## 2 The Beginnings of Faith

**Make sure you know the following:**
- An essential part of being human is asking questions.
- Asking questions means that we are interested in learning more about a particular topic. The questioner is the one who looks for this information.

- **Our search for meaning:** To **search** is to look at what is around us. **Meaning** refers to a sense of purpose. It is something that has importance and significance for us.
- When we ask questions about the meaning of life it is a sign of maturity. We begin to look at life at a deeper level. Finding meaning gives us a sense of purpose. Without it life can seem **meaningless**.
- In our search for meaning we can turn to many sources:
  1 **Family:** Our family can have a big influence on us. People find love and encouragement from their families and this can give them a sense of meaning.
  2 **Friends:** Friends are there for us in the good times and the bad. Without friends we would be lonely and isolated. Therefore, friendship brings meaning to our lives.
  3 **Music**: Music can bring meaning as it may help us to express what we are thinking and feeling.
  4 **Money:** Some people think that money will bring meaning to their lives. However, while it may make life easier it cannot buy us the important things like health and love.
  5 **Religion:** Religion can help people to understand major events in life such as birth and death. It can give meaning to the mysteries of life.
- **Awe and wonder:** Admiration and respect for something or somebody, perhaps after a great event.
- **Humanism/humanist:** A humanist's faith is not in God. It is in man. Humanists believe there is no God or Gods. They find meaning in how they respect and value life. They look to science for answers and want proof for their beliefs. They see things in a factual way rather than a spiritual way. They use reason and experience to make their moral decisions, rather than religious moral codes.

## 3 The Growth of Faith

**Make sure you know the following:**

- **Image of God:** This is a picture we have in our minds when we think of God. It is not just what God looks like but what kind of person or being we think God is.
- As we have never seen God our image may come from stories we have heard, pictures we have seen or songs we have listened to.
- Scripture can help us to form an image of God, especially passages such as the Psalms. In the Old Testament, Psalm 18 gives us an image of God as a rock, strong and secure: 'You are my mighty rock, my fortress, my protector, the rock where I am safe . . .' In the New Testament, Luke gives us an image of God as a shepherd who searches until a missing sheep is found.
- **Personal faith** is a person's own religious belief.
- **Stages of faith:** The growth and development of faith from childhood, through adolescence to maturity.

1 **Stage 1, Childhood Faith:** At this stage our faith is simple and trusting. It is influenced by those who teach and care for us. We do not really understand our faith but practise it as we see others doing.

2 **Stage 2, Adolescent Faith:** Can be a challenging stage. We are looking for answers and may feel that God does not understand us. We are influenced by friends and the media.

3 **Stage 3, Mature Faith:** The final stage of our faith development when we have reached a meaningful and comfortable relationship with God. We work at the relationship and know it is okay not to have all the answers to life but keep searching.

- Different people reach the different stages at different times.

# 4 The Expression of Faith

**Make sure you know the following:**

- **Prayer:** Prayer is a conversation with God whether in a formal or an informal setting. It is a way of sharing our lives with God.
- Prayer can give us support and comfort in times of trouble.
- **Prayer and music:** Liam Lawton is an example of someone who believes that singing is a way of praying. He works full time at writing sacred music for the Church in today's society. He uses music to reach out to people and to help deepen their relationship with God.
- **Worship:** Worship means giving God respect, honour and praise. Prayer is a form of worship. Through the sacraments we worship God publicly.
- **Information on people of religious faith:** For example, Mother Theresa, Maximilian Kolbe, Padre Pio, Gandhi etc.
- **Monotheism:** *Mono* means one and *theos* means God so monotheism is the belief in one God. Judaism, Christianity and Islam are examples of monotheistic faiths.
- **Polytheism:** *Poly* means more than one and *theos* means God so polytheism is a belief in more than one God. Buddhism and Hinduism are examples of polytheistic religions.

## Two examples of people of religious faith

**Frances Margaret Taylor**: Born into an English Anglican family in 1832. She nursed soldiers during the Crimean War. Some of the soldiers were Irish Catholics. She was so impressed by their faith that she became a Catholic herself. She believed that poverty could be material, moral or spiritual. She founded the Order of the Poor Servants of the Mother of God in 1869. She saw herself and her sisters as servants, as by serving they imitated Christ on earth. She established nursing homes for the elderly as well as schools. The sisters work in some of the poorest parts of the world today.

**Edmund Rice**: Edmund Ignatius Rice was born in Co. Kilkenny in 1762. His wife died after giving birth to their daughter. He was a wealthy man but became disturbed by the poverty some Catholics lived in. He began to pray and read the scriptures more. He decided to do something important for the children of Waterford and set up a school for boys. He really wanted to found a religious order of men who would educate these children and give them dignity and self respect. In 1808 seven men took their vows and not only educated the boys but fed and clothed them too. In 1820 the Order became known as the Christian Brothers. Many boys were given a better life because of Edmund Rice. The poor saw him as a man raised up by God. He was declared Blessed Edmund Rice in 1996 by Pope John Paul II and his feast day is the 5th of May.

# 5 Challenges to Faith

**Make sure you know the following:**

- **World view:** Our world view is how we see the world around us. It comes from everything we know from religion, philosophy and science.
- **Reflection:** When we reflect we think about something that is happening in our lives and try to understand how we feel about it. It is important to reflect on the existence of God.
- **Different responses to the existence of God: Theism** means to believe in God. **Atheism** means to deny the existence of God. For atheists God is not real. **Agnosticism** means the belief that the human mind is not capable of knowing whether God exists or not.
- **Secularism:** A secularist opposes the influence religion has on our society. Secularists make choices in life that exclude God.
- **Materialism:** A materialist believes that the only real things in life are material things that can be seen and touched. Therefore, they do not believe in a God. They consider that the scientific way of looking at things is the only way, as scientific truth is the only truth.
- **Religion and science:** The worlds of religion and science have a difficult relationship. For years people believed that you could not believe in both and you had to choose between them. These two worlds have differing viewpoints as the world of science is based on facts and concrete evidence, whereas religion is based on faith and trust.
- **Creation:** This is the story of how the world began.
- **Fundamentalism:** To believe in something literally or take it word for word is called fundamentalism. For hundreds of years people accepted the religious view of creation and took it literally. However, discoveries in the scientific world seemed to contradict what religion was saying.
- **The Big Bang:** A cosmic explosion billions of years ago that many scientists believe created the universe.

## The religious view of creation

The story of creation can be found in the first book of the Bible, Genesis. It speaks of God creating heaven and earth. He first made night and day, then heaven and earth. On the third day he made the seas, plants and trees. The fourth day saw the creation of the sun, moon and stars. On the fifth day he made birds and fish.

61

On the sixth day he made animals and male and female in his own image and likeness. Then on the seventh day God rested and made this a holy day.

## The scientific view of creation

**Galileo**: Galileo was an Italian astronomer from the 17th century. Using a telescope he discovered that the Earth orbits the sun. The Church became very concerned as his discovery contradicted what they had been teaching for years, that the Earth was at the centre of the universe. They banned his teachings. However, Galileo continued his work and the Church accused him of heresy. Heresy is an opinion that contradicts church teachings.

**Darwin**: Charles Darwin was a British scientist. He became famous for his theory of evolution. He discovered that all life forms – animal, plant and human – evolved over millions of years through a process called natural selection. They had all originally come from one organism. This theory contradicted the account of creation found in the Book of Genesis.

## Religion and science today

There is a much better relationship between the two worlds of religion and science today. People see that there are great lessons to be learned from both. Science is concerned with **how** the world came about whereas religion is concerned with **why** it did. Albert Einstein once said that 'Science without religion is lame, religion without science is blind.' Both have value and meaning in what they tell us about creation.

## Key Points

REVISE WISE
KEY POINTS

**Make sure you know the following:**

**1 The situation of faith today**
- Religious belief
- Religious practice

**2 The beginnings of faith**
- Life's questionings
- Search
- Meaning and meaninglessness
- Awe and wonder
- Humanism

**3 The growth of faith**
- Faith
- Personal faith
- Childhood faith
- Mature faith
- Stages of faith

**4 The expression of faith**
- Prayer
- Worship
- Monotheism
- Polytheism

**5 Challenges to faith**
- World view
- Reflection
- Atheism
- Agnosticism
- Secularism
- Materialism
- Fundamentalism
- Creation

## Sample Question and Answer

Here is a sample Higher Level question and answer from Section 4 of the examination paper.

## SEC Sample Draft Paper, HL, Section 4, Q4

A. a. Agnosticism is *the belief that the human mind is not capable of knowing whether God exists or not.* (6 marks)

   b. Give **one** reason why someone might hold this view. (6 marks)

*Someone may be agnostic as they may find it hard to believe in a God who they cannot see or touch. It makes it more difficult for people to believe that he is there.*

B. a. Listed below are a number of places and things to which people may turn in their search for meaning in life today. Pick **two** from the list and explain how each of them could help people to find answers in their search for meaning in life. (20 marks)

   Family          Music          Success          Relationships

*i. Music can help people to find meaning in life because sometimes the words of a song can express very well what they are feeling. Music can help people feel joy or sadness depending on the type of music it is. They can also use music when they are praying.*

*ii. A person's family can be a great help to them if they are trying to find meaning in life. A family gives love and support and accepts the person for who they are. They are also the ones who teach them about life and religion.*

B. b. Describe **one** difference between the secular humanists search for meaning and that of a person with religious beliefs. (18 marks)

*A person with religious beliefs will look to God and their religion when looking for meaning in life. They will see what guidelines their religion gives them about how to live their life and what is important in life. They may also go to their sacred scriptures and see what they say. These scriptures may give them hope and comfort. A secular humanist does not believe in God or organised religion. Secular humanists will look to other human beings and find their answers there. They would look to non-religious sources such as the Declaration of Human Rights.*

# Questions

## Section 1 Questions

### 2003, HL, Section 1, Q10

Reflection can be described as a human characteristic that involves a person thinking and becoming aware of his or her own feelings and actions (Tick the correct box). (5 marks)

True ☐ False ☐

### 2006, HL, Section 1, Q20

**One** factor which influences religious practice is _____
_____. (5 marks)

### 2005, HL, Section 1, Q19

Atheism holds the view that God exists (Tick the correct box). (5 marks)

True ☐ False ☐

### 2007, HL, Section 1, Q3

Polytheism is the belief in _____. (5 marks)

### 2007, HL, Section 1, Q17

Humanism holds the view that _____. (5 marks)

## Section 2 Questions

### 2003, OL, Section 2, Q3

This is a photograph of a young girl playing with a balloon.

A. Pick **one** thing from the photograph which suggests that this is an experience of awe and wonder for the girl. (6 marks)

B. Some experiences that might make a person react with awe and wonder are a birth, the beauty of nature, and music. What does the expression "awe and wonder" mean? (6 marks)

C. Experiences of awe and wonder make people ask questions about the meaning of life. Give an example of **one** such question. (8 marks)

### 2004, HL, Section 2, Q4

This is a photograph of young people holding candles.

A. Pick **one** thing from the photograph which suggests that this is an experience of reflection for these young people. (2 marks)

## Questions *(Continued)*

B. What is reflection? (2 marks)

C. Give **two** reasons why it is important for a person to have time for reflection.

(6 marks)

### Section 3 Question
### 2005, HL, Section 3

Read the following article and answer the questions below.

### Friend to the Dying

Two men are walking along a beach covered in starfish washed up by the tide. The younger man picks one up to throw it back into the sea. The older one says: "Why bother? It won't make a difference." The young man looks down at the starfish he's holding. "It'll make a difference to this one," he says.

This little story inspired Phil, founder of several hospices, to provide care for terminally ill children and young adults. Phil has spent the last 20 years working with children who have severe disabilities or who are dying. Every day Phil comforts people who have to go through the greatest pain that life can dole out. "It's the best way I know to live out my vocation," Phil says.

Many people find Phil's warm smile and calm way of speaking reassuring. But how was Phil drawn to this vocation? "Religion was a large part of my upbringing in Edinburgh," Phil explains. "My grandfather was very involved in our church. Later on, I worked in Great Ormond Street Hospital for Sick Children before moving to an adult ward in a nearby hospital. One of the patients I was looking after was a vicar who invited me to a service at her church. There I got to know people who had followed their vocation and had become members of a religious community."

"Some years later I was on a pilgrimage and I suddenly knew for certain that I should join a religious community. My family didn't like my decision and thought I would be wasting my life. But when Helen House was opened, the first ever place to offer special care for children who were dying, my mother appreciated what I was doing."

"Working in Helen House is not about being an expert," Phil says. "It's about companionship and kindness. After 21 years I have fewer answers to the big questions of life than I had at the outset. But what the experience of working with children has taught me is that, regardless of your belief or lack of it, when you're caring for people you are walking on holy ground."

*Adapted from The Sunday Times*

## Questions *(Continued)*

1. From your reading of this article outline **two** things that may have influenced Phil's religious belief. (10 marks)
2. Outline **two** ways in which Phil's life has been changed by his/her religious commitment. (14 marks)
3. "When you're caring for people you are walking on holy ground." Explain in your own words what you think Phil means by this. (16 marks)
4. Mature faith                       Inspiring vision

   How does this article show what is meant by **one** of the above terms? (10 marks)

## Section 4 Questions

## 2006, OL, Section 4, Q4

A. a. All human beings ask questions. Give **two** examples of important questions that a person asks in his/her search for meaning in life. (8 marks)

   b. The questions young children ask are often different from those asked by teenagers. Explain why this is so. (10 marks)

B. Which of the following gives non-religious answers to questions about meaning in life? (Tick **one** box only) (10 marks)

Humanism ☐                   Monotheism ☐

Tick **one** of the following world religions you have studied:

Buddhism ☐        Christianity ☐        Hinduism ☐

Islam ☐            Judaism ☐

Describe how religious belief had an effect on the life of an important person in the story of the world religion you have ticked above. (12 marks)

## 2007, HL, Section 4, Q4

A. People sometimes have experiences which make them wonder about the meaning of life. Describe how an experience in life could make a person ask questions about the meaning of life. (20 marks)

B. a. Materialism ☐                Secularism ☐

   Tick **one** of the above and describe what it means. (10 marks)

   b. Explain how the religious faith of a person could be challenged by either materialism or secularism. (20 marks)

## Section 5 Questions

## SEC Sample Draft Paper, HL, Section 5, Q4

You have been asked to write an article for a local youth magazine about the religious belief and practice of people today. In your article include information on the following:

The pattern of religious belief and practice among people today.

## Questions *(Continued)*

Things that influence the religious belief and practice among people today.

Comparisons between the religious belief and practice among people today and that of people in the past.                    (70 marks)

### 2003, HL, Section 5, Q4

Imagine you have been asked to talk, at a parent's night in a primary school, about the difference between the faith of a child and that of a teenager. Outline the talk you would give describing **two** things that could influence the way in which a child's faith might develop into a more adult faith.                    (70 marks)

## Your revision notes

# Section E: The Celebration of Faith

**●●●Learning Objectives**

**In this chapter you will learn about:**

1   Ritual and worship as part of the human response to life and the mystery of God
2   How communities of faith express their day-to-day concerns in various forms of ritual
3   The experience of worship
4   Exploring the link between patterns of worship and mystery and that which is of ultimate concern to individuals and communities

## 1 The World of Ritual

### Places of significance

- When a place has a special meaning or importance, it can be described as a **place of significance**.
- This place can be important if a group of people like it or memories are special about that place.
- Places can become significant for religious reasons. These places are called **places of pilgrimage**.

People go on pilgrimages to:

- Strengthen their relationship with God.
- Learn about their religion.
- Ask for help, guidance and forgiveness.
- Show devotion to God.

These activities can be called **actions of religious significance**.

### Places of religious significance

**Croagh Patrick**

- Croagh Patrick is in County Mayo.
- It has been a sacred place since ancient times.
- Christian tradition says that St. Patrick went up this mountain and spent forty days praying, fasting and reflecting there.
- Pilgrims come from all over the world to pray at this sacred place.

- Many make the trip barefoot as a sign of devotion.
- The first station is at the base of the mountain where the pilgrims walk around a mound of stones seven times, saying seven Our Fathers, seven Hail Marys and one Creed.
- The second station takes place at the summit and has four different stages. The pilgrims walk around the area known as Patrick's Bed seven times, again saying seven Our Fathers, seven Hail Marys and one Creed.
- The third station takes place at Roilig Mhuire where the pilgrims pray at the mound of stones repeating the sequence of seven Our Fathers, seven Hail Marys and one Creed. Finally they walk around the whole enclosure of Roilig Mhuire praying.

## Lourdes

- Lourdes is a place of religious significance in France.
- In 1858 a young girl named Bernadette saw a vision of the Virgin Mary there. She was only 14 years old at the time.
- The vision continued to appear for the next six months.
- At first people doubted her but after much investigation her experience was found to be true.
- Today millions of people travel to Lourdes to visit this sacred place to see for themselves where the visions took place and to pray for healing.
- Many people bathe in the water from the grotto and as a result there have been genuine cases of people being miraculously cured.

## Significant buildings – a Catholic church

- People show great respect in these buildings of significance. They can be described as sacred or holy places. A sacred place is where people feel close to God and it helps them to focus on their spiritual lives.
- The **altar** is where the celebration of the Eucharist takes place.
- The **ambo** or lectern is where the priest or Ministers of the Word read the sacred readings from.
- The **presider's chair** is where the priest sits during the mass.

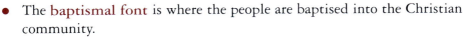

### Points to note

The priest is called the **presider** because he is the one who leads the congregation.

- The **baptismal font** is where the people are baptised into the Christian community.
- **Statues** of Our Lady and different saints are often found in churches.
- **Candles** are often found in front of the statues. People light them as a symbol of the prayers they say.

- The **Stations of the Cross** are found on the walls of the church depicting scenes from the crucifixion and the last important moments of Jesus life.
- **Stained glass windows** show colourful images of bible scenes.
- The **confessional box** is where people receive the sacrament of reconciliation.
- At Christmas time there will be a **crib** in the church. This is built to look like a barn and depicts the story of Jesus' birth.

## Times of religious significance

Certain times have become significant for religious communities. This is because an important event that took place in history may be set aside to remember an important person in religion. The Christian community has its own calendar called the **liturgical calendar**.

### Advent

The liturgical year begins with the season of Advent which means 'the coming'. It lasts for four weeks leading up to Christmas.

### Christmas

During Christmas we celebrate the birth of Jesus Christ. The 25th of December is a holy day of obligation. This means that Christians should go to mass.

### Ordinary Time

This falls into two parts of the liturgical calendar: the first between Christmas and Lent and the second between Easter and Advent. During this time we learn from the gospels about the miracles Jesus performed and the parables that he told.

### Lent

Lent for Christians takes forty days. This does not include Sunday. Lent recalls the time that Jesus spent in the wilderness before embarking on his public ministries. Lent is a time to prepare for Easter. The last week of Lent is called **Holy Week**.

### Easter

This is the most important time in the liturgical year. This was the time when Jesus died on the cross and rose from the dead so that all people could have the chance to share eternal life with God. Easter is celebrated on a Sunday between March 22nd and April 25th. The celebration begins with a vigil mass on Easter Saturday night.

# 2 Experiencing Worship, Sign and Symbol

## Experiencing worship

On pilgrimages people communicate with God. It also helps them share their lives with others in a special way. This expression of deep love and affection that we have for God is called worship. Worship may take time but it has many rewards. People worship differently, but for Christians the greatest kind of formal and community worship is in the celebration of the Eucharist or mass.

At mass:

- People gather together in communal prayer and thanksgiving for God's love.
- We ask for forgiveness for the sins we have committed.
- We listen to the word of God through the readings.
- We receive the body and blood of Christ.
- We are then sent out to the wider community to show love and to serve God.

## Ritual

- A ritual is a religious ceremony that involves a series of actions that are performed without any variation. Many Christians take part in rituals when they gather as a group to worship God.
- Rituals are symbolic actions that help people express their beliefs, values and concerns. They help people become closer to God as they allow people to celebrate the presence of God in their lives.
- They serve as a way of communicating what is important to people and what has meaning for people in their lives.
- Rituals are not routines – rituals have a symbolic action that allows there to be a link between the person worshipping and God.

## The mass

- Many people attend mass on a regular basis.
- At the Last Supper, Jesus and his disciples celebrated the Jewish Passover meal with bread and wine. In the Jewish Passover the blood of the lamb that had been sacrificed and put on their doors saved people.

## Points to note

To **sacrifice** something means to give it up for the good of something that is more important.

- Jesus sacrificed himself on the cross for us.
- The Eucharist is the greatest act of worship for Catholics.
- The word Eucharist means thanksgiving. We are thankful to God for giving us life — for our creation. Jesus' death on the cross meant that each of us could be saved from sin.

### The order of the mass

There are four different parts to the mass:

1. **Introduction:** We are welcomed to the mass.
2. **Liturgy of the Word:** The Word of God is spoken from the Bible.
3. **Liturgy of the Eucharist:** We receive the body and blood of Jesus in the form of bread and wine.
4. **Conclusion:** We are blessed and sent forth in the knowledge that we are safe in the hands of God.

### Participation

- At mass we are called to **participate** or take part in something.

## Points to note

**Participation** means to be involved in the activities of your local church and doing everything with the grace and dignity it deserves.

- In **baptism** we are called to take our rightful place in the Church.
- As lay people we can actively participate in the readings, prayers of the faithful, offertory or we can give out Communion. We can also become involved in the music of the mass.
- When we participate we understand more clearly the message of Jesus Christ and therefore can go forward and spread the good news.

## Sign and symbol

- A **sign** is an action, word or picture that gives a single message. A sign is used to pass on information.
- A **symbol** can be used when we find it difficult to put into words what we want to say. It is an action, word or picture that gives a message but is different to a sign. It can have many meanings and the power to affect people.
- **Icons** are sacred pictures that are painted on wood. The word itself means 'image' in Greek.

## Sacraments

A **sacrament** is a religious ceremony in which participants receive the grace of God. God's love for us is communicated in a very special way through the sacraments. All sacraments are communal celebrations.

### Sacraments of initiation

Through these sacraments we become full members of Christ's body here on earth.

| Sacrament | Type | What it celebrates | Meaning | Primary words and symbols | Ongoing effect |
|---|---|---|---|---|---|
| Baptism | Initiation | Welcome and rebirth | Being born into new life in the community of Jesus | Water, white garment, lighted candle, signing of the cross, anointing with oil | Membership of the church, call to witness |
| Confirmation | Initiation | Growth in the spirit | Strengthening of new life | Laying on of hands, anointing and sealing with chrism | Completes baptismal grace, call to witness |
| Eucharist | Initiation | Jesus' saving death and risen presence in our midst | Remembering Jesus' death and experiencing his real presence | Bread, wine, words of consecration | Deeper relationship with Christ, spiritual nourishment |
| Reconciliation | Healing | Forgiveness | Repairing broken relationship with God, others, and church | Confession of sins, words of absolution, laying on of hands | Liberation from sin |
| Anointing of the Sick | Healing | God's healing love | Living the fullness of life in Christ, even in sickness and death | Laying on of hands, anointing with oil, words of petition | Strength, peace, courage to endure |
| Marriage | Vocation | Covenant of love | Forming a bond of union, like that of Christ and the church | Husband and wife, rings, vows | Permanent union of a man and a woman |
| Holy Orders | Vocation | Ministry in the Church | Taking responsibility for a particular leadership role | Laying on of hands, anointing with oil, prayer of priestly consecration | Sacred powers for service to the church |

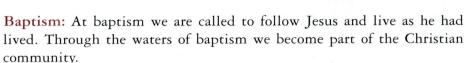

## Points to note

**Initiation** means to become a member of something.

**Baptism:** At baptism we are called to follow Jesus and live as he had lived. Through the waters of baptism we become part of the Christian community.

**Confirmation:** At confirmation we receive the gifts of the Holy Spirit through the oil of the chrism.

**Eucharist:** On our Communion day we celebrate receiving the body of Christ for the first time with the Christian community.

### Sacraments of healing

Healing is not just a physical thing; it can also be a spiritual matter as Jesus forgave the sinners for their wrongdoings.

**Reconciliation:** When we receive God's forgiveness for our sins, we are filled with the strength to continue to live as Christ wants us to live.

**Anointing of the sick:** In this sacrament the risen Jesus is present to heal and strengthen the person who is ill.

### Sacraments of vocation

In the sacrament of holy orders and marriage we are called to live out the message of Jesus Christ on earth.

**Holy orders:** Sacraments of vocation are special ways that we are called to serve by God. Priests serve the people of God on earth by preaching the Gospels and giving the sacraments.

**Marriage:** Through the sacrament of marriage two people are called publicly to make a covenant or promise to love each other for the rest of their lives.

### Sacrament of baptism

- Baptism is a ceremony of welcoming.
- It establishes the infant's identity as part of a church community. Identity is important as it gives ownership of something to all.
- Water is an important symbol in baptism as the pouring of water on the baby's head symbolises new life to the infant. The priest names the child at this stage giving him/her their identity.
- The oil has many healing qualities. The anointing of the new Christian with oil on the head signifies being the chosen one.
- The candle symbolises the bringing of the light of Christ into the child's life.
- The white garment symbolises that the one anointed shares in the resurrection of Jesus Christ. This infant is now a 'new creation' of Christ, ready to set out on a new journey.

# 3 Worship as a Response to Mystery

- Different experiences make people wonder about the mystery of life.
- Mysteries like that of birth, life and death are difficult to explain.
- They can be described as an ultimate concern in life.
- They are important life-changing events and they can make people reflect and wonder. People can think deeply about the event and ask questions about the meaning of it.
- When people are sick they often question the existence of God. It is something to celebrate that God is always close by, guiding us through the rough times.
- Through the sacrament of anointing we encounter the risen Jesus as God is present to heal and strengthen the person who is sick.
- Through this sacrament the community are united as one – they communicate through the sacrament. They pray together and join together in supporting the sick person and his/her family.

# 4 Prayer

- Prayer is something that is part of all religions.
- Prayer is a conversation between God and human beings.
- Every relationship needs communication to survive. Prayer is a way of keeping a good relationship with God.

## Types of prayer

1   Penitence: This prayer is to say sorry for something that we did that was wrong.
2   Praise and thanksgiving: This prayer is to thank God for the lovely things he has given us.
3   Petition: This prayer is when we ask God for something for ourselves.
4   Intercession: This prayer is used when we ask God to help others.

## Ways of praying

1   Personal prayer: When a person prays alone and has a personal and private conversation with God.
2   Communal prayer: When people gather together in a sacred place and share prayers with others.
3   Singing: When we sing we 'pray twice'. We are using the gifts that God gave us to pray.
4   Meditation: When we become quiet and focus our thoughts on God.
5   Contemplation: When we use no words but simply sit and concentrate on God.

## Formal and informal prayer

Formal prayer: These prayers are a set pattern of words that are familiar to the community of faith, for example the Hail Mary or the Our Father.

**Informal prayer:** We ourselves make up the words to pray to God. Often people have difficulties praying as there may not be enough time in the day, there may be too many distractions or they may find it hard to pray to a God they cannot see.

**Person of prayer:** Saint Maximilian Kolbe understood the importance of prayer. He was a priest in the Franciscan Order. In 1941 he was sent to Auschwitz Concentration Camp as a prisoner. He felt that God had sent him there to give spiritual strength to the other prisoners. He prayed with the other prisoners and often gave his own food to others. He spoke words of love to all. One day a prisoner escaped. As punishment, ten prisoners were to be shot. Maximilian offered to take the place of a man who had a wife and family. While waiting to be shot he said prayers and sang hymns with the prisoners. He gave them great strength. Moments before his death, he could be heard praying. In the face of hatred and death he prayed with great faith to God.

Other important people of prayer include St Theresa of Avila and St Ignatius of Loyola.

## Key Points

**Make sure you know the following:**

### 1 The world of ritual
- Places of significance
- Actions of significance
- Times of significance

### 2 Experiencing worship, sign and symbol
- Worship
- Ritual
- Participation
- Sign and symbol
- Icons
- Sacraments
- Identity
- Communicating experience

### 3 Worship as a response to mystery
- Encountering mystery
- Reflection
- Wonder
- Encounter with God
- Communication

### 4 Prayer
- Communication with God
- Penitence
- Praise and thanksgiving
- Petition
- Intercession
- Personal prayer
- Communal prayer
- Meditation
- Contemplation

## Sample Question and Answer

Here is a sample Ordinary Level question and answer from Section 4 of the examination paper.

## Sample Question and Answer

### 2003, OL, Section 4, Q5

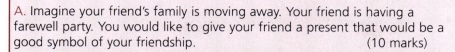

A. Imagine your friend's family is moving away. Your friend is having a farewell party. You would like to give your friend a present that would be a good symbol of your friendship. (10 marks)

*The present that I would give to my friend if she was going away is a photo album of the happy times we had together.*

Explain **two** things about your friendship that the present symbolises.

*i. This present symbolises a lot. It symbolises the happy times we had together during the last few years as I always went on holidays with her family and we had great times exploring where we went.*

*ii. The photo album also symbolises the close bond that we share as we have been through some difficult times together and we still are best friends.*

B. Below are pictures of objects used in prayer and religious rituals.

Scrolls of the Torah
*Transedition Ltd & Fernleigh Bks*

Statue of Buddha
*Articles of Faith*

Cross
*Saint Mary's Press*

Prayer Mat
*Flame Tree Publishing*

Statue of Shiva
*Saint Mary's Press*

a. Pick any **two** of these objects and explain why each is important in a world religion. (15 marks each)

*i. For Christians the cross symbolises the death of Jesus Christ and His Resurrection on Easter Sunday. Jesus caused quite a stir as he went about his public mission. He was unlike any previous preacher that had gone before him. Crucifixion was a brutal death*

## Sample Question and Answer *(Continued)*

at the time. At 3 o'clock, when darkness covered the land Jesus cried out in a loud voice "Father into your hands I command my spirit". These were His last words. Jesus became a martyr.

*ii.* The Scrolls of the Torah are very important to the Jewish faith. It is their most important sacred text. The sacred text is a result of a long process which began with the spoken word. It is believed to have many writers as there are different styles of writing and some repetition. It is so sacred that it cannot be touched. A special pointer is used to read it. The scrolls can be stored in a wooden case or are sometimes covered with beautifully embroidered cloth.

## Questions

### Section 1 Questions

1. A prayer of penitence is a prayer which expresses sorrow for sin.
   True ☐                              False ☐
2. Baptism is an example of a Christian sacrament. Name **one** other example.
3. Name **two** types of prayer.
4. Why is praying difficult for some people?
5. Worship involves activities in which God is honoured.
   True ☐                              False ☐

### Section 2 Questions
### 2003, HL, Section 2, Q4

This is a photograph of a group of people praying.
A. State one thing from the photograph which suggests that these people are expressing their religious faith.          (2 marks)
B. Give two reasons why a person might express his/her faith in this way.          (4 marks)
C. Participation is part of worship. State how participation can be seen in this photograph.
          (4 marks)

### Section 3 Questions
### 2003, OL, Section 3

After reading newspaper articles on the Russian Orthodox Church in Ireland a student decided to visit the church during Sunday worship. The following is a page from a project that the student wrote afterwards.

## Questions *(Continued)*

### My Visit to a Russian Orthodox Church

St. Peter and St. Paul's Church,
Harold's Cross Road, Dublin

Icon

The first thing I noticed is that there are a lot of icons inside this church. The first icon I saw was right in the middle of the church. I was told that when people come in they take a candle to this icon. Then they bow and kiss the icon. They touch their foreheads against the icon, and some parents will lift their children so that they, too, can touch the icon. There are other icons on the windowsills. The next thing I noticed is that there are very few seats. This is so that people can easily walk from one icon to the next.

The priest celebrates the "Divine Liturgy" behind a special wooden screen. This screen has icons of Jesus, Mary, and the Angels. There is a gate in the middle of the screen. This is to remind people of the gateway to Paradise. Behind the screen there is a small altar and a small table. You can see the priest at the altar if you look through the gate.

## Questions *(Continued)*

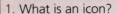

1. What is an icon? (10 marks)

2. From your reading of this project page select **two** other objects and explain why they are used in a place of worship. (12 marks)

3. Describe **two** rituals from this project page which show that icons are important to members of the Russian Orthodox Church. (20 marks)

4. Imagine that you have been asked to design a painting in the style of an icon for a prayer/reflection room. Name **three** things you would include in your design. Explain how each of these things would help people to pray/reflect. (18 marks)

## Section 4 Questions
### 2003, HL, Section 4, Q5

A.

| Statement Number 1 | Statement Number 2 | Statement Number 3 |
| --- | --- | --- |
| "Every human person is a mystery, which must be learned slowly, reverently, with care, tenderness and pain, and is never learned completely." - Anon | "I can see nothing plain; all's mystery. Yet sometimes there is a torch inside my head that makes all clear, but when the light is gone I have but images…" - W. B. Yeats | "A mystery is not a wall against which you run your head, but an ocean into which you plunge. A mystery is not a night; it is the sun, so brilliant that we cannot gaze at it…" - E. Joly |

a. Which of the above statements best describes encountering mystery in life? Explain your choice. (10 marks)

b. People often look back on life and recognise the experience of mystery at certain times and in certain places. Identify **one** life experience and explain how it could hold a sense of mystery for a person. (15 marks)

B. a. Sometimes people give expression to the experience of mystery through worship. Describe **one** example of worship in which people express their experience of mystery in life. (10 marks)

b. Explain how this act of worship helps people to express their experience of mystery in life. (15 marks)

### 2004, HL, Section 4, Q5

A. a. Name a type of prayer associated with **one** of the following world religions: (6 marks)

Buddhism    Christianity    Hinduism    Islam    Judaism

## Questions *(Continued)*

b. Give **one** example of the type of prayer named above and explain how it illustrates that type of prayer. (10 marks)

c. Explain how the type of prayer named above illustrates **one** belief of the world religion you have chosen above. (14 marks)

B. Below are pictures of gestures and positions people sometimes use in prayer.

Pick **two** gestures or positions and explain what each symbolises when used in prayer. (20 marks)

*Bowing*

*Joining hands*

*Kneeling*

*Sitting*

*Standing*

## Section 5 Question
### 2006, HL, Section 5, Q5

**Communal prayer and worship show what a community believes and values.**

Discuss this statement referring to **one** community of faith you have studied. (70 marks)

## Your revision notes

# Section F: The Moral Challenge

●●●**Learning Objectives**

**In this chapter you will learn about:**

1    The human need to order relationships at personal, communal and global levels
2    How this need can be expressed in a variety of ways
3    How this need is expressed in civil and other legal codes
4    How religious belief is expressed in particular moral visions
5    The moral visions of Christianity and one other major religion
6    The impact of these visions on the lives of believers and non-believers in considering some current moral issues
7    Aspects of the relationship between religion, morality and State law

## 1 Introduction to Morality

### What is morality?

**Points to note**

**Morality** is knowing what is good and bad behaviour and making decisions on this basis.

- Every person has a sense of morality, regardless of their race, age or religious background.
- The decisions that we make affect the people around us in different ways.
- People can have different reasons for deciding what is moral:
    1  Feeling guilty.
    2  Fear of being caught.
    3  The laws of their country.
    4  The laws of their religion.
    5  Gut instinct.
    6  Following the crowd.
    7  Obeying orders.

- Each of us makes choices every day. A moral choice is making a decision about what is right and wrong. These choices not only affect us as individuals. They can also affect the society that we belong to and the wider world.

- Because we live in a society where human beings live together, our morality affects those around us; therefore, we can say our morality is personal and communal.

- We have different kinds of relationships with people and sometimes the decisions we make can even affect people we do not know.

- We need to take responsibility for our actions as the choices we make are not always the right ones and therefore they may have consequences.

- Often people feel they have the right to do as they please. As human beings we are free to make choices in our lives.

- As Christians we believe that God gave us this right to have free will. With this right comes responsibility.

- Often people or groups of people can influence the decisions we make. The main influences are:

  1  Family.
  2  School.
  3  Media.
  4  Friends.
  5  Our church.
  6  Our community.

## 2 Sources of Morality

### Points to note

To **source** something is to find out exactly where it has come from.

Our morality comes from a number of sources that help to shape us into the people we will become. These sources are:

1  Home and family.
2  Peer groups.
3  School.
4  Religion.
5  The State.

### Home and family

- The family provides moral standards, education, religious background, love, security, customs and cultures. If we are taught good values in the home we will learn to be respectful to others throughout life.

- Parents are the primary educators of their children. They instil in their children good values that will stand to them throughout life.
- Talents are nurtured and nourished in the home.
- Stories of the family are passed from one generation to the next which helps form our characters. Every family has its own identity.
- The love that a family shows to each other is unconditional. The story of 'The Prodigal Son' (Luke 15: 11-31) is evidence of that.

## Peer groups

### Points to note

A **peer group** can be defined as a group of people the same age.

- All young people want to belong to a peer group and they feel anxious when excluded from the activities of the group.
- Friends are important as they can help us become better people.
- Adolescence is a time when we have to stand on our own two feet and make decisions for ourselves without being pressurised into doing something by the group.
- Often the decisions we make can leave us 'out in the cold' from the group.
- Real friends treat each other with respect and listen and care for each other. They are supportive of each other.

## School

- The school is a community that works together to help support each other.
- Young people spend a lot of time in school so it is important that they work together to make the community a good place to be. This means showing respect to all people in the community.
- At school we can be influenced by others or we can influence them. Therefore, school is an important place that can shape the people we become in later life.

## Religion

- Most world religions have a moral vision. A moral vision will shape the decisions and choices we make. Our moral vision can often be influenced by our religious beliefs. Most religions have a moral vision.

### Points to note

A **moral vision** is to see the difference between right and wrong.

- For Christians the most important ideal is the teachings of Jesus Christ given to us in the sacred scriptures such as the Bible. For the followers of Islam their sacred scriptures are the Qur'an.
- Christians worldwide have been guided by the Church on moral issues. By listening to the Church and reading the scriptures we become more informed and therefore can make correct decisions.

## The State

- In Ireland we live in a Democratic State. This means the people of Ireland (at eighteen years of age) elect representatives to Dáil Éireann to represent us in government.
- The elected government makes the laws for the country that each citizen must obey. These laws protect us.
- In March 2004 the government introduced a law in Ireland banning smoking in public places. Anyone who fails to abide by this law is fined. Most people do not want to be fined so they abide by all laws.

## Moral rules and guidelines

- A law is a rule that prevents us doing the wrong thing or making the wrong decision on a particular matter.
- Principles help shape our behaviours and influence the moral decisions we make. A principled person would not allow another person to be treated unfairly.

### Points to note

A **principle** is a law that one holds to be right.

- In school we follow a set of rules or codes and this helps in the efficient running of the school. It also helps safeguard the well-being of each student.
- It is often difficult to sum up one's moral code but the word 'love' is a very strong one in the Ten Commandments. Here, we are told to love God with all your heart, all your mind and all your strength.
- Throughout scripture we hear Jesus telling us to 'love one another as I have loved you' or 'treat others as you would like to be treated.' Jesus showed love to all people, especially the outcasts of society.
- An example of someone who demonstrated moral vision is Christina Noble. Her love for the street children of Vietnam is evident in the work that she does there. Today she is often referred to as a Mother Teresa!

## Laws

- Some codes and principles are formal. They have been put together for a reason. Formal codes tend to be written down and must be accepted by everyone. Formal rules are put together over a period of time.
- Other rules are described as informal as they are often unofficial and not written down. They often depend on the goodwill of people.
- All laws are specific but each law is based on the underlying moral vision. When driving, wearing a seatbelt, not speeding and not drink driving can save people's lives. Putting others first is something that we have learnt from scriptures.

## Religious moral vision

- A person with a religious moral vision understands that each and every person is made in the image and likeness of God and each of us is unique to Him.
- Because of this moral vision, there is a yearning to live by God's message of 'Love your neighbour as yourself'.
- One example of such a person is Sister Stanislaus Kennedy. Her religious moral vision is deeply rooted in scripture. The respect and love she shows to those who are homeless and who have no voice in society through her work with Focus Ireland is evidence of this.

## Authority

- Another aspect to codes and principles is authority.

### Points to note

REVISE WISE
POINTS TO NOTE

**Authority** means to have a certain power or to be highly knowledgeable about a certain subject.

- Many people look to their religion as an authority to help and guide them when making moral decisions or forming a moral vision.
- For Christians this authority comes from two sources:
  Scripture: Religious people see their sacred text as a direct link with their God and because of this they see it as a special authority.
  Religious leaders: Jesus gave special authority to the Apostles to continue his work on earth. Peter was given most of the authority. Jesus said Peter would be the rock on which he would build his Church. Peter went on to become the first pope of the Church. This authority given by Jesus has been handed down to each pope right up to today. Religious people look to the authority of their leaders when making a moral decision.

## Tradition

- Another aspect to codes and principles is tradition.
- Tradition is a continuing process through which the Church reflects on the teachings of Jesus and passes this from one generation to the next.
- An example of a tradition of the Catholic Church is to give up something for Lent.
- Tradition grows and develops over time.

## 3 Growing in Morality

### Moral growth

> ### Saint Ignatius Loyola – an example of moral growth
>
> Saint Ignatius Loyola was born in Spain in 1491. When he was young he loved gambling and fighting. This all changed when he was injured in a battle with the French when he was thirty years old. He began to read some religious books, which made him begin to question his life. He decided to devote his life to the service of God. To do this he needed more education in theology and philosophy. After some time he set up a group of priests called the Companions of Jesus (Jesuits). In 1622 he was canonised a saint.

### Stages of moral growth

**Children:** All moral growth is gradual. As children we learn very quickly that something is right or wrong. We learn a lot from our guardians. Our morals are based on rewards and punishments. What we learn as children influences our behaviour at the time and also later in life.

**Adolescence:** As we move into adolescence we understand very quickly the difference between right and wrong. We grow in maturity. The peer group has a major significance in our lives because its approval of what we do is fundamental to our being. We want to be trusted and so feel the need to assert our independence. The adolescent looks to rules and laws for guidance.

### Moral maturity

- A morally mature person takes into consideration the feelings of others and bases their morality on what they hold to be true.
- Society expects people to grow in maturity as well as physically, emotionally and intellectually. This does not always happen.

- When you reach moral maturity you move from selfishness to altruism. To be altruistic means you think of others before yourself when making a decision. This is very important to society.
- A morally mature person is aware of their responsibility to respect the rights of others and think of the consequences of the decisions they make.

## Conscience

- The word conscience comes from the Latin word 'to know'.
- Some people see conscience as their inner voice telling them what to do in a situation. But people must be careful as this inner voice might tell us to do something wrong.
- The Catechism of the Catholic Church teaches us that conscience is a law that we must obey because it is written in our hearts by God. Conscience is our ability to know, using our judgement and knowledge, what is the right and the wrong thing to do in a situation.
- An informed conscience means that one has all the facts on the matter before a decision is made.
- A religious person would inform their conscience by reading their sacred text or by speaking to a leader from their religion.

# 4 Religious Morality in Action

## Moral decisions

Making moral decisions can be described as a process. There are two parts to this process:

1 Asking questions, for example, what are my options, what might be the consequences for me, who will be affected by my decision and how might others be affected?

2 Finding answers, for example, what does my conscience tell me, what would my parents and friends think, what does my religion tell me and what does the law say about it? When making a moral decision we must take into account all aspects of the decision, not just part of it.

## Justice and peace

The struggle for justice and peace is one of the most important ideals of a Christian moral vision. However, it is not exclusive to Christianity as it is shared by all churches who work continually for justice. Throughout scripture we are asked to follow the teachings of Jesus Christ and to act justly towards our neighbour. Jesus clearly identified with the poor, the sick, women and the downtrodden during his ministry. There can never be real love of God without loving others. Scripture says justice should be central to all our lives.

### Glencree: centre of peace and reconciliation

The Glencree Centre puts justice and peace to its forefront. It was founded in 1974 in reaction to the violent conflict in Irish society. People wanted to believe there was a better way than violence, intolerance and sectarianism. Reconciliation was the way forward. The centre welcomes all traditions in Ireland that have the same hopes in peace building. It works in the areas of education, recreation and fundraising.

## Stewardship

Being a steward means looking after and protecting all of creation. It calls on us to be responsible for the decisions we make about how we use the earth and its resources. We are caretakers of the earth and of each other. A Christian religious moral vision calls on us to be stewards of creation because we believe that God made the world in his own image and likeness. As a result we are called to act as stewards to all living things and to show respect for all forms of life. We are all familiar with the slogan Reduce, Reuse, Recycle. This statement applies to all major world religions:

1 **Christianity:** Care for the environment is a big part of Christianity's moral vision. Jesus spoke about his love for nature in his parables and teachings. In 1988 the Catholic Bishops of the Philippines published the first pastoral letter on the environment called, 'What is happening to our beautiful land?'

2 **Judaism:** The Jewish sacred texts tell us that God created the earth and every living thing on it. The Book of Genesis contains the creation story, which explains how God created the world in seven days. God also created human life to live side by side with these creations. So humans are seen as a part of nature.

3 **Islam:** The Qur'an gives guidance on how Muslims should view the natural world. Muslims see humans as having a privileged position as guardians of the earth. Islam has a strong sense of the goodness and purity of the earth. The colour green is the most blessed of all colours for Muslims.

4 **Buddhism:** Buddhists strive to live in harmony with one's body, nature and other people. All life is precious and all life is connected. Buddhists have compassion for all living things.

5 **Hinduism:** Hindu's sacred texts contain imagery that values the power of the natural world. The River Ganges plays an important role in their

89

beliefs and worship. Mahatma Gandhi preached about the importance of living a simple life in harmony with the earth.

We can see that all of the major world religions have a similar moral vision when it comes to the care of the earth. It could be said that this vision is based on the principle of stewardship.

## Sin and reconciliation

When we do something wrong we are committing a **sin**. Sin has traditionally been divided into two types:

- **Venial:** Less serious, such as disobeying your parents.
- **Mortal:** This is seriously wrong, for example murdering someone.

When we sin we turn away from God or another person and damage our relationship with God and others. If we genuinely want to change our ways and rebuild our relationship with God we can turn to the sacrament of reconciliation. True reconciliation is not achieved by just tolerating those who may have hurt us, but by actively embracing them in love and welcoming them back into our lives. **Forgiveness** of sin should be at the heart of all Christian beings. The greatest example of forgiveness is when Jesus said on the cross, 'Father forgive them, they know not what they do.'

For **reconciliation** to fully happen there has to be an action. The relationship that has been broken needs to return to where it was before the offence took place. Reconciliation is the restoration of relationships as it welcomes the offender back into the life of the offended. This may be one of the most difficult things we are asked to do as Christians. Pope John Paul II welcomed the man who shot him back into the family of God, thus reminding the whole world that God has welcomed us back. His moral vision was steeped in the faith of Jesus Christ. In the Jubilee Year in 2000 the Pope encouraged his followers to embrace the ministry of reconciliation.

## Sacrament of Reconciliation

Reconciliation is about bringing the Christian community closer together and closer to God. It heals any hurt that people feel and in doing so makes it easier for people to love again without any barriers.

In the Sacrament of Reconciliation we are given the opportunity to meet the risen Christ. Through his forgiveness we are encouraged to move forward with ourselves and our neighbours. The sacrament can be seen as a healing of relationships that have been broken. Through sin we turn away from God but through reconciliation we are allowed to turn back into the palm of his hand.

The priest offers us forgiveness on behalf of the community when our confession is heard. During confession the act of contrition is recited whereby the confessor thanks God for all the love he shows us and promises not to sin again. After this the priest gives an absolution and the person is cleansed from sin.

# 5 Religious Morality and State Law

## Points to note

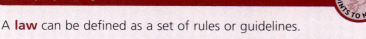

A **law** can be defined as a set of rules or guidelines.

Laws allow people to live in a safe and secure environment. Laws inform people about what is acceptable behaviour in a country or state. Very often these laws reflect the laws of our religion. They complement our personal morality, e.g. the **State law** says it is against the law to take another person's life and the Ten Commandments in Christianity state, 'Thou shall not kill'.

The rulers of a country use a set of guidelines to help them when making the laws of the land. This is known as the constitution.

## Personal morality versus State law

Sometimes conflict occurs between **personal morality** and State law, e.g. a person's religious morality leads them to be against abortion yet the country they live in allows or legalises abortion.

### Pluralism

A **pluralist** is someone who holds the view that the laws of the state should not be influenced in any way by the laws of a religion. They believe that society is made up of people from all different races, cultures and religions and each should be as important as the other. They believe that all people should be able to live together in one peaceful society. Religion and State law should be kept separate.

### Religious fundamentalism

**Fundamentalism** could be described as the opposite of pluralism. Fundamentalists are people who believe that the teachings, beliefs and writings of their religion should be taken word for word. These teachings should not only be the laws of the religion but also the law of the land.

### Libertarianism

A **libertarian** is someone who values the freedom of the individual above all else. They do not agree with the state having any influence on the moral lives of it's citizens.

## Key Points

Make sure you know the following:

### 1 Introduction to morality

- Morality
- Relationships
- Choice
- Freedom
- Influence

### 2 Sources of morality

- Moral vision
- Laws
- Religious moral vision
- Authority
- Tradition

### 3 Growing in morality

- Moral growth
- Moral maturity
- Conscience

### 4 Religious morality in action

- Decision making
- Justice
- Peace
- Stewardship
- Respect
- Forgiveness
- Reconciliation
- Sin

### 5 Religious morality and State law

- State law
- Personal morality
- Pluralism
- Religious fundamentalism
- Libertarianism

## Sample Question and Answer

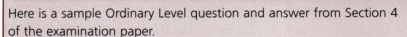

Here is a sample Ordinary Level question and answer from Section 4 of the examination paper.

### 2003, OL, Section 4, Q6

"I have decided that, if all else fails, I will fight. I believe it is the right thing to do."
Person X

"I believe in peace so I have decided that I will never fight."
Person Y

A. Read the two quotes above. Describe the thoughts person X **or** person Y might go through in order to reach this decision. (15 marks)

*Person X has decided that if all else fails they will fight as this is the right thing to do. They may feel they have no other choice.*

B. a. Give **one** example of a situation where peace is under threat. (5 marks)

*Peace is under threat in Northern Ireland even though there is a power-sharing agreement between Ireland and Britain.*

## Sample Question and Answer *(Continued)*

b. Taking the example you have given, suggest **two** things a religious leader might say/do to promote peace in this situation. (20 marks)

*Religious leaders have promoted peace many times in the North.*

*i. The religious leaders of the North have actively involved themselves in the peace talks over the years. They have always been supportive of political leaders involved in the peace process.*

*ii. A religious leader like Aidan Troy has always been supportive of the two communities living in the North of Ireland. At one stage he got caught up in the difficult situation of Catholic children being prevented going to their school as they had to go through a Protestant estate to get to their school.*

## Questions

### Section 1 Questions

1 What does behaving morally mean?
2 In religious tradition what does reconciliation mean?
3 Religion can be described as a source of morality in a person's life. Name one other source of morality.
4 Morally mature people think only of themselves in making decisions.

True ☐                False ☐

### Section 2 Questions

### 2006, HL/OL, Section 2, Q3

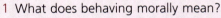

1 I am the Lord your God: You shall have no other gods before me.
2 You shall not make wrongful use of the name of the Lord your God.
3 Remember the Sabbath day and keep it holy.
4 Honour your father and your mother.
5 You shall not murder.

6 You shall not commit adultery.
7 You shall not steal.
8 You shall not bear false witness against your neighbour.
9 You shall not covet your neighbour's house.
10 You shall not covet your neighbour's wife.
Ex. 20:3, 7, 8, 12, 13-17.

**This drawing shows a moral code.**

## Questions *(Continued)*

A. Explain why this is an example of a moral code.

(4 marks)

B. Name one religious moral code. (2 marks)

C. Give two reasons why a moral code is important in a community of faith. (4 marks)

### 2004, HL/OL, Section 2, Q2

This is a photograph of a newspaper headline describing a road accident in which the driver of a car killed a person and drove away.

A. State **one** way in which the situation described in this headline shows the need for respect. (2 marks)

B. State **two** ways in which the driver could be affected by his/her decision to drive away. (4 marks)

C. State **two** ways in which society could be affected by the driver's decision to drive away. (4 marks)

### Section 4 Questions
### 2003, HL, Section 4, Q6

Imagine you are on a train with a woman and a man sitting opposite you. During the journey the woman leaves her seat without taking her bag. A moment later you see the man getting ready to leave the train with the woman's bag under his coat.

A. Describe **two** different ways of dealing with this situation. (21 marks)

B. Explain the consequences of **one** of the above ways of dealing with this situation for each of the following: (15 marks)

The Woman                    The Man                    Yourself

C. Explain how a person's religious moral vision could influence his/her decision-making in this situation. (14 marks)

### 2005, OL, Section 4, Q6

A. a. Moral issues arise in situations where people have to make decisions about the right thing to do. Tick the box that shows the moral issue arising in each situation below. The first situation has been matched to a moral issue as an example for you.

# Questions *(Continued)*

### Situation 1

Two of your friends have a row and are not speaking to each other. You get tickets to a concert and bring them both to it. The row is soon forgotten and they enjoy the concert together.

The moral issue involved in the situation is – (Tick the correct box)

### Situation 2

You have seen a classmate taking another student's schoolbag without permission. The student whose bag has been taken asks if you know anything about the missing bag. You have to decide what to say.

The moral issue involved in this situation is – (Tick the correct box)

### Situation 3

You are organising a class outing to the cinema. One of your classmates uses a wheelchair. You discover that the bus with wheelchair access will cost more. You have to decide whether to go ahead without this classmate or do more fundraising so that no one will be left out.

The moral issue involved in this situation is – (Tick the correct box)

| | | | | | |
|---|---|---|---|---|---|
| Truth | ☐ | Truth | ☐ | Truth | ☐ |
| Justice | ☐ | Justice | ☐ | Justice | ☐ |
| Authority | ☐ | Authority | ☐ | Authority | ☐ |
| Reconciliation | ☑ | Reconciliation | ☐ | Reconciliation | ☐ |

A.  b. Explain how **one** of the moral issues ticked above arises in the situation it is matched with. (10 marks)

B.  Outline how a morally mature person would decide what is right or wrong in any **one** of the situations described above. (12 marks)

C.  Explain how a person's religious beliefs could influence his/her view of right or wrong in any **one** of the situations described above. (10 marks)

## Section 5 Question

Show how a community of faith in today's world can help its members to respond to a situation in which truth or peace may be threatened.

# Your revision notes

# Journal Work Checklist

- The journal work part of the exam is worth 20% of your final mark, so remember it is worth doing well.
- It must be submitted on an official booklet or journal so it may be useful to complete a draft one first for practice.
- It can be completed any time during the three-year Junior Certificate cycle but must be submitted by a certain date given by the State Examinations Commission. This is usually some time during the last school term before the Junior Certificate examination. You can find detailed information on this on the State Examinations Commission website, www.examinations.ie
- Remember to write your exam number clearly on the front cover of the journal booklet and indicate what level you are doing by ticking the Ordinary or Higher Level box.
- Ensure that you write out the full official title in the first section of the booklet. This can be found on the State Examinations Commission website.
- Make sure you stay focused on the title throughout. When your journal is complete, read back over it and ask yourself if you have referred directly to the title in each section.
- You may find lots of interesting information while doing your journal work. However, you only have a limited amount of space in the booklet, so decide what the most important information is and keep it clear and to the point.
- Do not forget to use the prompts down the side of the booklet as they will help focus you on what to write.
- Do not make the mistake of being too general. For example, if you are doing journal work on the importance of prayer in a world religion, describing what you saw on a visit to a place of worship in that religion is not enough. Remember to keep the information relevant to the title at all times.

## Sample Question and Answer
### 2008, HL, Section 4, Q2

**A.** a. Each of the different religious groups described below lived in Palestine at the time of Jesus.

Tick ☑ the box that most correctly matches each description to the name of a religious group given below. The first description has been correctly matched to the name of a religious group as an example for you.

| *Religious Group 1* | *Religious Group 2* | *Religious Group 3* |
|---|---|---|
| We are wealthy aristocrats and have strong links with the Temple in Jerusalem. We accept Roman rule and have power in Palestine. | We reject Roman rule in Palestine and are ready to fight the Romans. | We do not co-operate with the Romans. We run the local synagogues and are strict about keeping all the laws of Judaism. |
| The name of the religious group which matches this description is – (Tick the correct box) | The name of the religious group which matches this description is – (Tick the correct box) | The name of the religious group which matches this description is – (Tick the correct box) |
| Pharisees ☐<br>Sadducees ☑<br>Zealots ☐ | Pharisees ☐<br>Sadducees ☐<br>Zealots ☑ | Pharisees ☑<br>Sadducees ☐<br>Zealots ☐ |

b. ☐ Pharisees     ☐ Sadducees     ☐ Romans

Choose **two** of the above groups and explain why each came into conflict with Jesus.        (14 marks)

*A b. i. Sadducees: The Sadducees were a wealthy group who held the powerful position of High Priest in the Temple. When Jesus overturned the tables in the Temple they became annoyed as they did not want things to change. Temple worship gave them money and power. They wanted to get rid of Jesus before it was too late.*

## Sample Question and Answer (Continued)

*ii.* **Pharisees:** The Pharisees thought Jews should follow the religious laws over everything else. They lived their whole lives by it. They became very angry with Jesus for healing people on the Sabbath and eating with tax collectors, which they said broke the laws. He told parables that showed them up.

**B.** a. Give **two** reasons why the Sanhedrin was important in Palestine at the time of Jesus. (14 marks)

B a. *i.* The Sanhedrin were very important in Palestine. The Romans were the ones in charge but they let the Sanhedrin act as a kind of religious court. They gave them a certain amount of power over the Jews in Palestine. This helped keep the peace in the land. They even had their own guards in the Temple.

*ii.* The Sanhedrin were able to punish people who broke the religious laws. They could not put anyone to death but they could punish them harshly; the people knew this and were wary of them. As there were so many religious laws they were a powerful group.

b. Outline what happened when Jesus was brought before the Sanhedrin. (14 marks)

b. Jesus was brought before Caiaphas, the High Priest. They needed to find some charges against him so they could get Pontius Pilate to put him to death. They brought false witnesses against him and it was held at night so it was not a fair trial. They found Jesus guilty of blasphemy, which means claiming to be as great as God. They decided to hand Jesus over to Pontius Pilate who would have the power to kill him.

## Sample Question
### 2008, OL, Section 4, Q5

**A.** a. Croagh Patrick is a place of religious importance for a community of faith in Ireland. Name **another** place in Ireland that has religious importance for a community of faith. (8 marks)

b. Explain **two** reasons why the place you have named above has religious importance for a community of faith. (12 marks)

**B.** a. Describe **one** example of a ritual that can be seen in an experience of worship that you have *either* taken part in *or* observed. (10 marks)

b. Explain **two** reasons why people use religious rituals to express their faith. (10 marks)

# Key Definitions

## Section A

| | |
|---|---|
| Authority: | Being responsible for others/having power. |
| Church: | A community of believers. |
| Commitment: | Being dedicated to something. |
| Community: | A group of people with something in common. |
| Community breakdown: | When a community collapses due to a lack of co-operation, communication and sharing. |
| Communication: | Sharing and discussing ideas with others. |
| Co-operation: | To help others and make compromises for the good of the community. |
| Denomination: | Belonging to a particular branch of a religion. |
| Ecumenism: | Christian churches working together to achieve unity and understanding. |
| Gospel: | Good news/New Testament books. |
| Identity: | The unique characteristics of a person or group. |
| Interfaith dialogue: | Different world religions working together to achieve understanding and respect. |
| Inspiring vision: | That which motivates people to believe in something. |
| Leadership: | Guidance given by those in a position of authority. |
| Ministry: | The work a person does within their community or faith. |
| Mission: | Putting our religious beliefs into practice. |
| Preaching: | Spreading the message of God. |
| Religion: | Belief in and worship of a God or Gods. |
| Roles: | The parts people play in a community. |
| Sectarianism: | Hatred or discrimination of another person because of their religious belief. |
| Service: | Doing something for others. |
| Sharing: | Giving of yourself to others. |
| Tolerance: | Accepting others regardless of their beliefs. |

Vision: What a community sees as important and central to their work.

Vocation: A calling to serve God.

# Section B

Ancient Judaism: The history of the Jewish people, including politics, culture and religion.

Conflict with authority: The tension between Jesus and those in power, such as the Pharisees.

Discipleship: Following the call of Jesus in thought, word and deed.

Eucharist: A thanksgiving meal which is celebrated by Christians. It is one of the sacraments in the Catholic Church.

Evangelist: One of the four Gospel writers: Matthew, Mark, Luke and John. They were people of faith.

Evidence from oral to written tradition: How information about Jesus went from the spoken to the written word.

Gospel: Stories of Jesus' life that are found in the New Testament. The word means good news.

Kingdom of God: A way of living based on Jesus' message of truth, justice, peace and love.

Martyrdom: Being willing to suffer and die for your religious beliefs.

Memorial: Something that is done to remember and honour the memory of someone or something.

Messianic expectation: The Jewish people were awaiting a messiah (a redeemer), who would free them from Roman rule and establish a new Jewish kingdom.

Miracle: An amazing event performed by Jesus that showed the power of God.

Missionary: Continuing the work of Jesus on earth.

Parable: A short story told by Jesus to teach the people about the Kingdom of God. The story is based on earth with a message about heaven.

Passover: The festival celebrated by Jews to remember the events that led them to freedom.

Pentecost: The event marking when the Apostles were given the gift of the Holy Spirit.

People of God: Those who believe in God and try to carry out his will.

Presence: Jesus' presence (existence) after the resurrection was an everlasting one.

Resurrection: Jesus was restored to life three days after he had died.

Sacrifice: Being willing to give up something for the sake of others.

| | |
|---|---|
| Synoptic: | The Gospels of Matthew, Mark and Luke are called synoptic because they present or make the same point of view. They have great similarities. |
| Table fellowship: | Jesus chose to share his meals with all to show that God's kingdom was for everyone. |
| The Holy Land: | The region where Jesus lived, preached and died. At the time it was known as Palestine. |
| The Roman Empire: | All the lands that Rome ruled at the time of Jesus, including the Holy Land. |
| Transformation: | The change that occurred in Jesus after the resurrection, making him alive in a new way. |
| Vocation: | A calling to serve God. |
| Witness: | To see and give evidence about something. |

# Section C

## Islam

| | |
|---|---|
| Allah: | The name given to God in the Islamic faith. |
| Beliefs: | Core or central ideas of a religion, which give its identity and often affect the lives of the believers. |
| Caliph: | The chief Muslim civil and religious leader. Also, the successor to Muhammad. |
| Convert: | A person who changes from one particular religion to another. |
| Cultural context: | How people lived in a particular place at a particular time. |
| Festival: | A special time set aside by a religion to celebrate a certain aspect of the religion, in a particular way. |
| Five Pillars of Faith: | Shahadah (creed); Salah (prayer); Zakah (charity); Sawm (fasting); Hajj (pilgrimage). |
| Founder: | A person who starts or sets up something from the very beginning. |
| Hafiz: | A person who can recite the entire Qur'an. |
| Hajj: | A pilgrimage to Mecca that every Muslim should make once in their lifetime, if they are able. |
| Halal: | Meat that has been prepared in a certain way, so as to allow all the blood to drain out of the animal. |
| Haram: | Things that are forbidden in Islam. |
| Hijra: | The event that took place in 622 CE where Muhammad and the Muslims left Mecca. The Islamic calendar begins from this date. |
| Imam: | The leader of an Islamic community. |

Islam: The religion meaning peace by submission or obedience to the will of Allah.

Mosque: The Islamic place of worship.

Muhammad: The founder of Islam.

Muslim: A convert to Islam, meaning someone who has accepted the message of Allah.

Pilgrims: People who have made a special journey for religious reasons.

Polytheists: People who believe in and worship many gods.

Prophet: A person called by God to receive an important message and preach it to the people.

Qur'an: The sacred text of Islam, which Muslims believe is the word of Allah.

Ramadan: The month of fasting in Islam.

Revelation: A vision or dream through which God makes himself known to a person and reveals or presents information to them.

Rite of Passage: The events used to mark a person's journey through life.

Schism: A split or a divide in a religion.

Shi'a: A group of Muslims who believe that anyone who takes over leadership after Muhammad must come from the same family as him.

Sunni: A group of Muslims who believe that the only true leadership comes from the Qur'an itself and how it has been interpreted by scholars.

**Buddhism**

Buddha: A name that means 'Enlightened One' and which was given to Siddhartha Gautama by his followers.

Buddhist: Someone who takes refuge in the Buddha, in his teachings and in the Sangha.

Different forms of Buddhism: Theravada; Mahayana; Vajrayana.

Meditation: A communal type of prayer that can be done on its own or in a group led by a leader. For Buddhists meditation is not a conversation with God, but a way to control their mind and help them make the right choices in life.

Middle Way: The theory founded by Siddhartha Gautama which states that people could find happiness in a life lived between extreme luxury and extreme hardship.

Nirvana: A state of perfect happiness and peace or enlightenment. It is seen as ultimate salvation.

| | |
|---|---|
| Relic: | An object that belonged to a holy person, which is kept and treated as holy after their death. |
| Sangha: | A community of monks and nuns founded by the Buddha. |
| Siddharta Gautama: | The man who founded the religion called Buddhism. |
| Stupa or pagoda: | A monument in a temple which holds the relics of the Buddha of the temple. |
| The Eightfold Path: | The Buddhist way of life. |
| The Four Noble Truths: | Duktha, Samudaya, Magga and Nirvana. |
| Tripitaka: | The sacred writings of Buddhism, which mean 'Three Baskets'. |

## Judaism

| | |
|---|---|
| Ark: | A special cupboard in the synagogue where the scrolls of the Torah are kept. |
| Bar Mitzvah: | A ritual that occurs when a Jewish boy is seen as an adult in his faith. It means 'son of the commandment'. |
| Bimah: | This is the raised platform in the synagogue from where the Torah and prayers are read. |
| Covenant: | A special agreement between God and his people. |
| Covenant of circumcision: | A special ceremony that takes place when a newborn baby boy is circumcised as a sign that he is entering into the same covenant with God that Abraham did. |
| Diaspora: | The scattering of the Jews from Israel after it was taken over by the Romans in 70 CE. |
| Hebrews: | The name by which the Jewish people were known when they lived in Israel before the birth of Judaism. |
| Kaddish: | A special prayer for mourning said by Jewish people. |
| Kiddushin: | The Hebrew name for marriage. |
| Kosher food: | Food that is clean and pure, and meat that is slaughtered in a certain way. |
| Main beliefs of Judaism: | Monotheism; Identity; Covenant. |
| Monotheistic: | A religion in which people believe and worship only one God. |
| Ner Tamid: | A light that always hangs above the ark in the synagogue. It is constantly lit and symbolises the everlasting covenant with God. |
| Oral Torah: | Discussions on the written Torah that are contained in three texts: the Mishah, the Talmud and the Midrash. |
| Orthodox Jews: | Jews that are very traditional and follow the Torah closely. |

| | |
|---|---|
| Patriarch: | A founding father. Abraham was the first patriarch. |
| Persecution: | When a person is evicted from a place, hurt or even killed because of their religious beliefs and opinions. |
| Polytheistic: | A religion in which people believe and worship many Gods. |
| Promised Land: | The place in Canaan chosen by God, which was to be the home of the Jewish people. |
| Rabbi: | A religious leader in the Jewish faith, also called a scribe. |
| Rites of passage: | Special ways of celebrating the important moments in life. |
| Rites and rituals: | Words or actions that are performed by Jews in a special way at a certain time. |
| Shema: | The most important prayer in Judaism. |
| Shiva, Sheloshim and Yahrzeit: | The three stages of Jewish mourning. Shiva is the first seven days of mourning; sheloshim the first 30 days after the burial; and yahrzeit the first 12 months after the death. |
| Synagogue: | A place of meeting. Jews use it as a place not only for worship but also office work, parties, study and meetings. |
| Tenakh: | The name Jewish people give to the Hebrew Bible. |
| The Holocaust: | The extermination of Jews by Adolf Hitler and Nazi Germany between 1933 and 1945. |
| The Western or Wailing Wall: | The most sacred place for Jews. It is the last remaining wall of the temple built for Jews in Jerusalem, which was destroyed by the Romans in 70 AD. |
| Reform Judaism: | Jews who do not follow the same strict laws as do Orthodox Jews. |

## Hinduism

| | |
|---|---|
| Arranged marriage: | When parents plan for their son or daughter to marry someone that they choose to be suitable. |
| Brahman: | The supreme soul or spirit that Hindus believe in, and which has no form. |
| Creed: | A summing up of what the followers of a religion believe in. |
| Dharma: | The Hindu belief to always do what is right and correct. |
| Garbagriha: | The shrine room where the statue of the God or Goddess is kept. |
| Guru: | A spiritual adviser in Hinduism. |
| Hindu festivals: | Three important Hindu festivals are Divali, Holi, and the Kumbh Mela. |
| Hindu Gods: | Brahma, Vishnu and Shiva. |

| | |
|---|---|
| Karma: | The belief that when you do good, good will come your way, and when you do bad, bad will follow you. |
| Puja: | The Hindu word for worship. |
| Religious festival: | A special time usually remembered by fasting or celebration. |
| River Ganges: | A river held sacred by Hindus. Many Hindus wish their ashes to be scattered in the Ganges when they die. |
| Samsara: | The cycle of birth and rebirth. It is also called reincarnation. |
| Sanskrit: | The language of Hindus. |
| Satyagraha: | A method of direct social action developed by Gandhi that is based on the principles of courage, truth and non-violence. |
| Upanishads: | An important Hindu sacred text that contains stories and parables, such as the Mahabharata and Ramayana. |
| Vedas: | The oldest Hindu sacred texts consisting of four collections of prayers, hymns and magic spells. |
| Yantra: | A design that helps Hindus to pray. |

# Section D

| | |
|---|---|
| Adolescent faith: | A challenging stage of our faith development when we ask many questions. |
| Agnosticism: | The belief that the human mind is not capable of knowing whether God exists or not. |
| Atheism: | To deny the existence of God. |
| Awe and wonder: | To be filled with curiosity and have an admiration or respect for something or someone. |
| Creation: | The story of how the world began. |
| Fundamentalism: | A literal interpretation of sacred scripture. |
| Humanism: | Humanists believe there is no God or Gods. They find meaning in how they respect and value life. |
| Humanist: | A humanist's faith is not in God, it is in humankind. |
| Materialism: | A belief that the only real things in life are material things, e.g. money or possessions. |
| Mature faith: | The final stage of our faith development when we have reached a meaningful and comfortable stage with God. |
| Meaning: | Meaning is something that has importance or significance for us. |
| Meaninglessness: | Meaning gives us a sense of purpose in life. When things become meaningless they are not important to us any more. |
| Monotheism: | *Mono* means one and *theos* means God, so monotheism is the belief in one God. |

Personal faith:      A person's own religious beliefs.

Prayer:      A conversation with God.

Polytheism:      *Poly* means more than one and *theos* means God, so polytheism is a belief in more than one God.

Question:      Asking questions means that we are interested to learn more about a particular topic.

Questioner:      The questioner is the one who looks for this information.

Religious belief:      Religious belief means the things that we believe to be true about God and the faith we belong to.

Religious practice:      Religious practice is how we show these religious beliefs. It means that we put into practice in our lives all that we believe.

Reflection:      When we reflect, we think about something that is happening in our lives and try to understand how we feel about it.

Search:      To seek answers or reasons for things around us.

Secularism:      This practice opposes the influence that religion has on our society.

Stages of faith:      The growth and development of faith from childhood, through adolescence to maturity.

# Section E

Actions of significance:      An action has significance if it carries meaning for the person.

Celebration:      Ceremonies to mark a special event in your life.

Communal prayer:      When we pray with others.

Communication:      To share or pass on God's loving message.

Communicating experience:      To pass on the teachings of religion from one generation to the next.

Communication with God:      When prayer is used as a way of keeping our relationship with God alive.

Contemplation:      A type of prayer where we clear our minds to become one with God.

Encounter with God:      To meet God or feel his presence around us.

Encountering mystery:      Experiences that make people wonder about the meaning of life.

Icon:      Sacred or holy images painted in a particular way that can help people to pray.

Identity:      The unique characteristics of a person or group.

| | |
|---|---|
| Meditation: | A type of prayer where we focus on God through deep thought. |
| Participation: | To become actively involved in something. |
| Penitence: | A type of prayer where we say sorry to God for any wrongdoings. |
| Personal prayer: | When we pray alone. |
| Petition: | A type of prayer that asks God for something. |
| Places of significance: | A place or building that has special meaning or importance for a group of people. |
| Praise and thanksgiving: | A type of prayer that gives thanks to God for all he has given us. |
| Reflection: | To think deeply about something. |
| Ritual: | A religious ceremony that involves a series of actions that are performed without any variation. |
| Sacrament: | A religious ceremony in which participants receive the grace of God. |
| Sacredness: | Something set apart as holy. |
| Sign: | An action, word or picture that gives a message. |
| Symbol: | Actions, words or gestures that can have a deeper meaning than a sign and evoke a response from people. |

# Section F

| | |
|---|---|
| Action and Consequence: | The things we do or say (actions) cause something else to happen (consequence). |
| Authority and Tradition: | To have authority means to have a certain power or to be highly knowledgeable about a certain subject. |
| Civil Law: | The rules of a country, which are put in place by those in charge. |
| Choice: | A moral choice is making a decision about what is right or wrong. |
| Conscience: | The ability to know what is right and wrong using judgement and knowledge. |
| Constitution: | The guidelines used by the authorities when making rules of law. |
| Decision-making: | The ability to make a decision on a matter whether it is the right one or not. |
| Forgiveness: | To stop feeling angry towards someone and move towards reconciliation. |
| Freedom: | We are free to choose when making a moral decision but are limited by our responsibilities to others. |
| Influence: | Something that affects our decisions. |

| | |
|---|---|
| Integrity: | Being modest and morally upright. |
| Judgement: | The ability to make a sound decision. |
| Justice: | To act justly and fairly towards others. |
| Laws: | A law prevents us from doing something wrong. The government makes laws for the country. |
| Libertarianism: | The belief that everyone should be free to do as they choose, so long as they do not interfere with the rights of others. |
| Moral growth: | This is a gradual process moving from childhood through to adolescence and into adulthood. |
| Moral maturity: | When someone is morally mature they take into consideration the feelings of others and base their morality on what they hold to be true. |
| Morality: | Knowing what is good and bad behaviour and making decisions based on this. |
| Moral vision: | To see the difference between something that is right and wrong. |
| Peace: | To be free of violence. |
| Pluralism: | The belief that groups belonging to different races or different political or religious beliefs can live together in peace in one society. |
| Reconciliation: | Actively embracing the person who has sinned against us and welcoming them back into our lives. |
| Relationships: | The connections we have to other people. |
| Religious fundamentalism: | Believing what the sacred text or laws of your religion say, word for word, i.e. literally. |
| Religious moral vision: | The ability to see that we are made in the image and likeness of God and this helps us shape our moral decisions. |
| Respect: | To have a high regard for something and so treat it with consideration. |
| Sin: | An act that breaks a religious code. |
| Society: | Human beings living together in a community. |
| Stewardship: | Being responsible for caring for all of God's creation. |
| Tradition: | Something that we pass on from one generation to the next. |
| Truth: | The state of being true to oneself and others and not telling a lie. |